"SUSIE...AIN'T SHE A DOOZIE? MY 'HAZEL' DAYS AND BEYOND"

BY JULIA BENJAMIN

"Susie...Ain't She A Doozie? My 'Hazel' Days and Beyond"

"Susie...Ain't She A Doozie? My 'Hazel' Days and Beyond"
By Julia Benjamin
© 2016, ALL RIGHTS RESERVED
No part of this book may be reproduced in any form or by any means, electronic, mechanical, digital, photocopying, or recording, except for inclusion of a review, without permission in writing from the publisher or Author.

Published in the USA by:
BearManor Media
P O Box 71426
Albany, Georgia 31708
www.bearmanormedia.com

ISBN: 978-1-62933-077-8
BearManor Media, Albany, Georgia
Printed in the United States of America
Book design by Robbie Adkins, www.adkinsconsult.com

TABLE OF CONTENTS

Introduction v
Chapter 1 - My First Seven Years 1
Chapter 2 – The Beginning of My Hazel Days 8
Chapter 3 - Being Susie Baxter 19
Chapter 4 – Acting More in the 1960s and 1970s 42
Chapter 5 – Happy in Hawaii, Unhappy at Home 47
Chapter 6 – Getting Back into Acting 53
Chapter 7 – Close Encounters of the Famous Kind 55
Chapter 8 – How Mom and Dad Met 58
Chapter 9 – Finding Romance and Disappointment 64
Chapter 10 – Losing Dad 68
Photo Gallery 71
Chapter 11 – My Big Fat Greek Sabbatical 112
Chapter 12 – Big Mistake in the Big Apple 114
Chapter 13 – The Attack and the Aftermath 118
Chapter 14 – Correspondence Chaos 127
Chapter 15 – More Letters, More Lawyers 134
Chapter 16 – More Shenanigans Before Closure 146
Chapter 17 – The End Isn't the End 174
Chapter 18 – Finally the Real End 179
Chapter 19 – One More Thing to Note 181
Epilogue 183

INTRODUCTION

My name is Julia Benjamin. I am five feet, three inches tall. Blue eyes. Long, blonde hair. 105 pounds. Just perfect for a career in show business, right? Well ….

The story that I am about to tell you is true. There are some names that need to be changed, not because the people are innocent and need to be protected. Rather, it's quite the opposite—they do not deserve any notoriety by me or by anyone else because they were evil, cynical, jealous and manipulative.

Then there are those true Hollywood peers and mentors for whom to work with was a gift. Those people I am proud to name.

I was a former child star/adult actress for over three decades. One year while I was a child, I was fortunate enough to be cast as a series regular in one of the most popular sitcoms on television, playing opposite one of the biggest stars in show business. I acted pretty regularly throughout my teens, twenties and thirties. I then worked in the financial industry doing many different tasks for fifteen years.

Currently, I live in Colorado with my son, who is a chef, and I travel around the United States signing autographs at many nostalgia conventions. I also teach acting and voiceover to young, aspiring people who want to break into the entertainment industry.

As you read my story, my hope is that you will recognize the obsessive, horrific behavior that was frequently around me, and if you ever find yourself in a situation that mirrors mine, please accept the tools and strength I write about here to get away quickly. I survived. Not everyone will be so lucky. Consider this instance. It's a Sunday morning in 1998 at 10. I'm forty-one years old and in bed watching the "Hour of Power." My son is asleep and the phone rings. My boss, who is new to the securities firm that I have been working at for over four years, is on the line, extremely agitated. He proceeds to tell me that his schedule for the upcoming week in

Seattle is all screwed up. I ask him why he is calling me, as I do not handle his schedule in Seattle.

My boss says that earlier in the week he was yelling at his wife, telling her not to go outside because she has a black eye. I ask him where she is now, and he tells me she is taking a nap. He then gives me some advice. "Don't bend over in a dog park to tie your shoe because you might get a black eye." OK. But still … why are you calling me?

Now, I had actively worked in the entertainment industry for the previous thirty-six years and had just made a lateral move within this investment firm. I was previously employed by this CEO for six months. He was not a tall man. I really didn't know if he had a "short man's complex," but I certainly received an education in it from him.

On a previous day, he locked the front door of his firm while we were alone for the afternoon and insisted I come into his office, telling me he wanted to talk with me. He then started to give me a back rub and proceeded to put his hand under my blouse and grab my left breast.

Why did he have a hard time keeping his hands off me? He stood too close, he was always finding a reason to touch me, he breathed all over me and he was always so sneaky. And he called at odd hours and days, always when his wife was away or asleep.

Before you ask why I didn't report him for sexual harassment, remember, he was a CEO and I needed the work, which is also the reason I didn't quit. I made the lateral move instead. Yes, in hindsight, I was wrong, but when you're over forty and you're not sure where you'll work next, you sometimes make bad decisions. Plus, I was a single parent with a child to raise.

His type of behavior is everywhere and not just restricted to show business and those so-called casting couches. By the way, I soon realized that while "short man's complex" may be hereditary, not every short man has this problem. My dad, who was one of the best casting directors in Hollywood, was only five feet, seven inches tall. In his case, it was the opposite—the women loved him, and not because he could make them stars.

But I'm getting ahead of myself. I'm trying to say that even once you're out of the business—and by this time, I was definitely out—some things will always be the same. To understand this better, we need to go back to when I was "in."

"Susie...Ain't She A Doozie? My 'Hazel' Days and Beyond"

CHAPTER 1 – MY FIRST SEVEN YEARS

FADE IN: SAN FERNANDO VALLEY, CALIFORNIA

I was born Julia Ann Benjamin on February 21, 1957, the second adopted daughter of Phil and Toni Benjamin. Three days after my birth I was brought home, a very old soul was I.

As a small child at three or four years of age, I was very happy. We had a beautiful three-bedroom house. It had a sunken den with a used brick fireplace and a large, enclosed used brick lanai with a huge backyard and swimming pool. My dad's roses were all around the back and front of the house; he just loved his roses.

I loved to play outside in the backyard with my dog Toddy, a pedigree beagle. He was so sweet. For hours, I would make mud pies using some of the bricks and pie tins from the garage. I'd decorate them with the orange berries from our trees and the flower petals from my dad's roses, then try to curl Toddy's ears with the pink sponge rollers from the vanity I had. When I wasn't making mud pies and curling Toddy's ears, I would push him around the backyard in an old creaky pale mint green doll crib. He was my best friend and a good sport.

I also loved all the monarch black and yellow butterflies in our backyard. I called each of them Willie, and they would often land on my two small fingers. Sometimes I would bring them into the house and let them rest on the TV tray, upon which I often colored. Then I would take them back outside to free them.

I would sometimes draw for hours while watching my favorite TV cartoons—*Beany and Cecil, Huckleberry Hound, Augie Doggie, The Flintstones, The Jetsons, Top Cat* and best of all, *Felix the Cat.* Other times I could be seen hanging onto my mother's leg while she washed or cleaned the house, smoked her cigarettes (it was fashionable then) and listened to the radio or TV.

As for my father, Phil Benjamin was a successful and well-respected casting director for many of the studios throughout his long career. Some of my parents' friends in the industry wanted to put me in the business. One lady was an agent named Jean Halliburton. She and her associate, Dorothy McGuire, kept asking them to let me go out on interviews, hoping that they would say "Yes." One day when I was about six years old, they actually did say "Yes"…under the condition that if I didn't get the job, they wouldn't ask again.

It was a commercial for Marx Toys—four little girls having a tea party. On the day of the interview, my mom constantly told me to be a good girl, avoid touching anything and remain very quiet. Well, good and quiet I sure was—so good and so quiet that the director called Jean and told her, "We love Julia, she's just perfect for this, but if she'll just open her mouth and say something or even smile, well, then she's got the job!"

I eventually opened my mouth and eventually smiled … and I eventually got the job. Turns out that I beat out between 60 and 70 other little girls on that first interview! More advice from my mom followed while we were filming. "Remember, Julia…don't take your eyes off the director." Thanks again, mom. I didn't take my eyes off the director, and finally the director came over to me. "Honey, why are you looking at me?" I told him my mom said to keep my eyes on him all the time. Well, instead of disciplining me (and my mom), the poor guy just did his best to hide all over the set so I wouldn't see him!

The shoot was a wonderful commercial with the four of us having a tea party, all dressed up in beautiful party dresses: one little girl in purple, the second in yellow, the third in blue, and me in a very simple little pale pink satin dress with white velvet brocade flowers and a round neck, with my hair up in a bun, spouting a small little satin bow. The tea was actually chocolate milk. There was only one problem: I was very allergic to chocolate and peanuts. So I learned very quickly how to pretend to sip the tea.

I so wanted to wear what the other little girls were wearing. Their dresses and petticoats were so frilly and fancy, and my dress was so simple and plain. But from then on, I would always be dressed in classic simple clothes and colors so as not to take away from my face, mostly my big blue eyes. This advice came from one of my mom's best friends at the studio, Edith Head, the famous wardrobe designer. She instructed my mom on what I should wear, because she noticed early on how blue my eyes were and how my face would be photographed at the studios. To this day, I dress very conservatively in a timeless sort of fashion.

The second job I did was something I would eventually do for a good portion of the rest of my career—a voiceover for a movie my dad was casting at 20th Century Fox called The Sand Pebbles. I went to a soundstage on the lot that had a small room built inside for ADR (Automatic Dialogue Replacement) or "looping," as it's called. This involves creating new audio recorded after a film has been shot, replacing what is already on the track for a variety of reasons. Typically, when there was loud background noise while it was first recorded, or if an actor didn't give the proper line readings on the set, they would be recorded again during the editing process.

I played the part of a little girl crying on screen for her mother not to leave her. I ended up really crying, with my mom acting as my coach, waving to me and moving away as I delivered my lines. My mom explained it all to me in advance, and I remember that it was recorded in just two or three takes. I was told my little performance was equal to that of a skilled professional! As I said, eventually I would go on to do hundreds of voiceovers throughout all of my childhood and many of my adult years.

At age seven, I began meeting and working with my first acting coach, Lois Auer. Lois lived at the very top of a hill off Van Nuys Boulevard in Sherman Oaks. It was a very steep ride up that hill. My mom knew I was very scared because one could never see the cars coming from the other direction down the hill. We would always recite the Lord's Prayer going up, no joke.

Lois had a huge, beautiful home that overlooked the entire San Fernando Valley, and she had the most magnificent dog named Garth, a beautiful big gray Weimaraner that I loved to play with every time I went for my lessons. How I adored this dog! When I came over, he would always just sit outside the window by the living room where Lois and I would work together until we were finished, so I could go outside to play with him.

Her backyard was very steep all the way down to the gate. Garth would help me get back up by letting me hold onto his collar. He'd pull me back up until we reached the top. By the time I finished playing with him, I always developed hives on my arms, but I didn't care. I felt like we understood each other. I would go back inside and wash my hands, and Lois would give me a small glass of cola. My mom usually took a nap on Lois' couch while we studied.

I was reciting Shakespeare (Macbeth) at age 7! This was also when I started extensive voice training. Lois had a wonderful son, tall and handsome. After my lessons, Lois and my mom loved to chat about what was going on in Hollywood, while her son would teach me how to play chess.

Now, there was a TV series in 1964 called Valentine's Day. It starred Tony Franciosa and Jack Soo (who would later co-star on Barney Miller). My agent Jean requested the sides for a guest role in which I would audition, that of Jennifer, a little girl (obviously). Not only did I get the part (I actually won out over Angela Cartwright!), but my performance also eventually got me recognized as the "most promising young newcomer in a series" by the Academy of Television Arts and Sciences!

This show filmed on the 20th Century Fox lot during the same time that my father was working on The Sand Pebbles. The night that I had won the part, my dad went into the show's casting office and nonchalantly said, "Hi boys. Can I have my daughter's script?" Up until then, they had no idea we were related, but everyone was delighted.

Shooting Valentine's Day was a great experience. Every morning my mom and I would meet my dad at the studio commissary for breakfast. We sat at the very back of the room in a big booth where I could see the beautiful restaurant with all the white tablecloths, napkins and silverware all clean and sparkling, and small, pretty bouquets of flowers as centerpieces. I ate silver dollar pancakes with boysenberry syrup every day during my shoot.

Because I was a minor, I required a stand-in to work on the set for me while I received the mandatory three hours of schooling per day with a tutor. The stand–in was actually a little person. Her name was Sadie, and she was exactly my height! I was just fascinated with her. She would play games with me in my dressing room. We talked about why she was so tiny and cute and why, to me at least, she looked so "old."

Sadie was very patient and explained how "little people" lived. She explained how they drove their cars, had scaled-down counters and cabinets customized in their homes and led normal lives with just some very minor adjustments. I met Sadie's husband—also a little person—and he showed me their car. Their gas and brake pedals were specially built extra-long so they could drive. I really liked that—I wanted to drive their car, too! Years later, the "Little People of America" became a much-respected organization to help establish public awareness for the plights and concerns of these wonderful individuals. It was started by one of the biggest little people in the industry, Billy Barty.

The part of Jennifer was a very big assignment for my first time in a television series. In the episode, titled "Momma Loathes Papa," my role was that of a really spoiled brat. Joyce Van Patten played my mother. I absolutely loved her. She would always bring me a big iced and decorated cookie (like a gingerbread man) from the bakery to eat during our lunch break.

As the sister of actor Dick Van Patten and an established actress of her own right, Joyce knew my dad and had been cast by him many times prior to my meeting her. I grew to realize that my daddy was a very important person, because everyone told me how much they loved him. It was like he knew *every* actor, and they knew him. He loved his job. Everyone also adored my mom, Toni.

During this episode, there was a scene where Tony spanked me because I was not only a bad girl, but I also had a fresh mouth. When we started filming our scene, he really did spank me (and hard)! My butt was so sore. Wonder if the new child labor laws would permit such a scene being filmed today?

Anyway, everyone on the set was crying at the end of the take—everyone! Me too (it hurt!), but not as much as Jack Soo. When the director yelled cut, Tony left the stage; he seemed very upset. When he came back, we hugged and everything was OK again. Still, Jack seemed the most bothered by the scene. He and I took a little walk, hand in hand. We both just bawled, eventually wiping all the tears from our eyes, before we finally did stop crying. And then Jack and I laughed a lot!

This shoot on the Fox lot actually took place during the week of Valentine's Day, and when Jack came back from his lunch break one day, he had what looked to me like a fifty-pound box of chocolates in his arms. It was huge and in the shape of a red heart, with red satin ribbons and pink frills all around it. It smelled heavenly. It was filled with wonderful, fresh chocolates. Every kind of chocolate you can imagine was inside this giant box, too big for me to carry for sure. What a terrible irony that I was allergic to it all, but I do remember sneaking a few pieces, then sneezing like crazy. But, hey! It was all mine.

Jack and I had a wonderful scene playing poker together, with Tony overseeing the game at his office in his house. I had all the chips on my side of the poker table, and Jack looked so bewildered! It was such fun to shoot. Jack and I actually played for real during and between the takes.

Many years later, I went on an audition at *Barney Miller*, where Jack was then a series regular. His health had started deteriorating. When I met with the casting director, I told her I had worked with Jack when I was very young. She appeared a bit skeptical and said something to the effect of, "Really? Well, let's go say 'Hi' to him."

We left the casting office and took the elevator down to the stage where the cast was rehearsing for the live show at the end of the week. As we walked down the ramp to the audience bleachers, I saw Jack sitting in the first row, watching the rehearsal. Hal Linden, sitting near him, looked up from his script at me and told Jack that he thought he might have a visitor, since Hal clearly didn't know me.

When Jack saw me, he leaped up, and we hugged and hugged. All he said was, "Baby, my beautiful baby!" and then proceeded to keep turning me around like a ballerina. I had grown from a sweet, happy talented seven-year-old to a young woman in her late teens, with long, light brown hair. But I have always been a size one or three, tiny and petite. What a thrill that he recognized and remembered me!

Before he introduced me to the entire cast of his show, he told me he never got over my scene with Tony...and then tears started rolling down his cheeks again! Jack then formally introduced me to Hal Linden, Max Gail, Abe Vigoda, Ron Glass and Steve Landesberg. By this point, everyone seemed to know who I was. They all mentioned how they adored my dad. It was amazing. They all hugged and kissed me, my hands and my forehead. Jack Soo obviously loved me, and they wanted him to know that they loved me too. What a wonderful, generous cast! I spent about fifteen minutes with Jack. We talked about Hollywood, my career and my dad.

When the casting director and I went back up to the office, she gently told me that Jack was dying. I was clearly upset. I went home and spoke about Jack at length with my mom and dad. Oh, and I didn't get the part. I don't even remember now what the part was, because Jack died very shortly after I was reunited with him. I'm just glad I got to see him again. I loved him very much. He was truly one of the nicest people I've ever met. His heart was bigger than that fifty-pound box of chocolates he gave me.

Getting back to Valentine's Day, when my episode aired on ABC a month after I filmed it, a colleague of my father's, a gentleman named Eddie Quinn, sent him the following letter, which I discovered many years later:

March 30, 1965
Dear Phil:

It's up to you whether or not you want to tell Julia that her performance on the Valentine's Day TV show last Friday night was just terrific! Honestly, I thought she gave a beautiful performance. I only hope a lot of producers and directors caught the show, too. If they did, then the calls should be coming her way. If she isn't "star" material, then I miss my guess.

My best to you.
Always,
Eddie

Eddie did not miss his guess. His letter certainly set the stage for what was about to follow.

FADE OUT

CHAPTER 2 – THE BEGINNING OF MY *HAZEL* DAYS

FADE IN: HOLLYWOOD, CALIFORNIA

The television series Hazel, starring the award-winning Shirley Booth in the title role, had just completed four successful years on NBC when, for reasons unbeknownst exactly to me, the show got cancelled early in 1965. CBS decided to pick up the franchise and air it on Monday nights starting in the fall of 1965 following a popular hit, The Andy Griffith Show. CBS was about to broadcast several of their prime time series in color for the first time (Andy Griffith being one of them), and because Hazel had been produced in color since its second season, this was really a no-brainer for CBS—a color program that had already established a viewing audience.

But CBS wanted some changes to attract younger viewers. There was obviously nothing they were going to do about Shirley—even though she was well into her sixties by this time, she was the star. So those changes meant making the family that Hazel worked for younger ... a lot younger.

That meant that Don DeFore and Whitney Blake were out as George and Dorothy Baxter. So were most of Hazel's crony friends. The only regular cast member besides Shirley that ended up being retained was Bobby Buntrock, who played George and Dorothy's son, Harold Baxter. After all, he was a kid (a 13-year-old by now, but still a kid).

It was decided that Hazel would go to work for George's much younger brother, Steve, a real estate agent who lived in another town, and his wife Barbara, a beautiful blonde. Harold would go with Hazel to his uncle and aunt's residence, while the "older" Baxters temporarily relocated—to Saudi Arabia! CBS really wanted those older Baxters far, far away, and of course, in television terms, "temporarily" actually means permanently!

To further reduce the median age of the new TV cast, the producers also decided to give Steve and Barbara Baxter their own young charge, an 8-year-old daughter named Susie. Needless to say, the casting department at Screen Gems was pretty busy during the spring of 1965. Newcomers Ray Fulmer and Lynn Borden were eventually signed as Steve and Barbara Baxter. As for Susie, it took six months before they chose me.

One evening during my group acting class, a call came in from my agent, Jean, who asked to speak with my mom. She proudly told her that I had won the role of Susie Baxter on Hazel. What a thrill! My mom, Lois and I all cried.

I had interviewed at least six times over six months with the producers before they made their final decision. Lois helped me study the sides for that last audition. She told me when I got to the end of the scene to throw my arms around one of the producers as if he were one of the actors (the scene called for it), and not just read the lines and sit in my chair. So I hugged the producer. That did it!

During one of the early meetings in the production office that I attended once I got the part, Shirley Booth stopped by as she was leaving the studio. She was dressed in a white poncho with frills and sunglasses, with a turban style hat around her hair. She had a big, white purse—such a class act. She came into the room and shouted, "Hi boys! Are we ready for season five of my show?" Of course, the whole room stood up. Everyone greeted her with so much love and respect.

Once the formalities were done, she wanted to know where "our new little star" was hiding. I said, "I'm back here." Everyone was standing in front of me, and she couldn't see behind them. Shirley walked over and extended her hand. I held mine out to her. We shook hands and she asked me, "Julia, are you ready for your new adventure in television?" I curtsied and replied, "Yes, Miss Booth, I am, and thank you for having me on your show." After some more pleasantries were exchanged, Shirley told me that she would see me again at CBS for our publicity photos.

Shirley was like that – it was always "our," "we," "us," never "me" or "I." Thinking back, I truly believe this is why our show was such a wonderful set on which to work. Shirley was always so relaxed and comfortable, and as a result, so were we. By this point, she had already won an Academy Award for Come Back, Little Sheba, plus Emmys and Golden Globes at least twice for playing Hazel. She was also the recipient of numerous other awards and honors, all richly deserved. This wonderful lady was also a part owner of the Hazel series, and she had a definite say in deciding that I was the right actress to play Susie Baxter.

A few days later, my mom and I arrived at CBS Television City at the corner of Beverly and Fairfax in Hollywood. It was time to take those publicity stills that Shirley told me about. I remember that my mom and I walked through the main door, and security had us sign in. We then walked down a very long corridor that was filled with photos of all of the current stars who had programs airing on CBS at the time. It was a museum by itself. My mom was patient enough to let me take the time to look at and recognize all of the actors in the photos.

We then reported to the room where the photo shoot would take place with the entire cast. This was my first encounter with my soon-to-be TV cousin, Bobby Buntrock. Shirley had already arrived, and the two of them greeted us when we walked into the room. Shirley, Bobby and I were the first to do the photos together. I remember for the first shot, I was sitting on Shirley's lap and Bobby stood next to us. He was so full of energy—a typical American boy. He teased Shirley, and she teased him right back. They loved to talk about baseball and cars. I just listened and laughed while the photographer worked with us.

I remember asking Shirley if I was too heavy because we sat for our stills for a couple of hours. She was so funny! She said that the stool wasn't as comfortable as her car, but she was OK, and we would get up and stretch during breaks in our shoot. After about an hour, we all started talking together. Shirley was telling us about the new car that the network just gave her, and Bobby started showing me all of his baseball cards. At one point, he looked at me and said, "Do you know how to act?" Shirley assured him that I could. She told him about my Valentine's Day episode that I had recently shot, and Bobby looked at me with a comical expression and said, "Was that you?"

From that moment on, we were friends, VERY good friends, and partners in crime on Stage 5 and the backlot at Columbia Pictures. We were never at a loss to find something amazing to do, even on our first break for the still shots at Television City. He took me around CBS. Our mothers followed, and he invited me to have lunch with him at our own table at the CBS commissary. My mom and Bobby's mom became fast friends too. They were both military women. My mom was a WAC, and Bobby's mom was a WAVE. That was all it took.

After lunch, we all went back to the photo shoot, and it was then that I met my TV mom (Lynn Borden) and my TV dad (Ray Fulmer) for the first time. Everybody was so excited, and Shirley looked so happy with her new cast. On the way home that day on the freeway, my mom and I were so happy and ecstatic for what would be our new family and home away from home for the next year. We sang and laughed. She kept telling me over and over again how thrilled she was to have met Shirley and what a great gal Maxine (Bobby's mom) was, what a great job I did, and how everyone had told her I was such a well-mannered little girl, so beautiful, and how overjoyed the studio was to have me in the new cast. I couldn't wait to tell my grandma, dad and sister all about my adventures for the day. Unfortunately, there would eventually be a lot of jealousy at home.

Every morning at 4:30, my mom would wake me up saying, "Rise and shine, it's time to go to work," and I was ready. I was so excited to go to Screen Gems because at the time, everybody that I adored was on that lot shooting too. When I went to the studio each day, I always had my "friends" with me—my skateboard with my stuffed bulldog Petunia tied to it, one of those three-feet long red snakes tied around my head, curlers and all, and my bag of toys, stickers, coloring books, crayons, markers, and pencils. Petunia would be in many of the publicity shots too.

Upon arrival to the lot, right after we passed security, we would first encounter the two film-cutting booths. They would be to the right on our way to Stage 5, where Hazel filmed. Once our series was in production, Tom, one of the film cutters, would let me look at the dailies from the previous day's shoot. I'd see the film on a small editor's screen, and he would use his foot to pedal through the film forward and reverse. Sometimes I got to see film from some of the other shows shooting on the lot.

Speaking of which, the first soundstage after the cutter's booth was where I Dream of Jeannie filmed. Usually in the wee hours of the morning, all of the stage "elephant doors" would be wide open, so one could peek in and see the big, bright, beautiful set they used on Jeannie—lots of pinks and purples, rose and red velvets, jewels, babbles, bangles, beads, glitter mirrors, chiffons, satins, and those pillows with the most gorgeous fabrics ever! By now you all know that I'm referring to the inside of Jeannie's bottle. What a sight to behold! That set had to be fifty feet high, and it looked like it was cut in half, so one could see the velvet couches, the mirrors, everything! But there was always a red velvet rope around the entire thing. It was a "hot" set—look, but don't touch. Boy, did I look!

Once in a while, I did get to see the beautiful Barbara Eden in her harem outfit, looking as gorgeous as she did on television. She was a close friend of my dad's and later they would work together on Harper Valley PTA. Once in a while she would wave to me and say hello. What a thrill that was!

Hayden Rorke, who played the ever-frustrated Dr. Bellows on the show, was another friend of my father's. Frequently, he would join Bobby, his mom, my mom, me, and our studio teacher, Catherine Denney, at the studio restaurant for lunch on Gower Street, just outside the main entrance. Sometimes when we finished, Hayden would walk me over to his stage so I could get a closer look at everything inside and what they were going to shoot that afternoon. He was an incredibly nice and kind man. So was the crew, and Bill Daily (Major Healey) —always so nice and so funny—and Larry Hagman (Tony Nelson). They all knew my dad. They always told me to say hello to him when I went home for the day. Both my dad and my mom were friends with Larry's mom, the wonderful Mary Martin. When my mom pointed out to me that Larry's mom was the Peter Pan we always watched on television back then, needless to say I was thrilled. I wanted her to teach me how to fly.

There was a small lunch/snack café that we would pass next on our way to the Hazel stage. It served your basic quick foods (chips, sandwiches, coffee and juice), and it was run by a wonderful woman named Delores. Everyone just adored her. She was always dressed in a pink waitress uniform with a white apron and a little frilly hat. Delores took care of the entire lot. We were all in and out of there so much during the day. The biggest memory I have is that it was the first place I can remember that had a microwave oven. My mom would buy me a Danish, and after it was placed in the microwave, it was so hot that it took a very long time for it to cool down just to open it!

The next stage on the way to ours was used for The Donna Reed Show, and that's where I met my longtime friend, Paul Petersen. By now, it was the eighth and final season of that series, and Paul was about twenty years old. I remember vividly seeing him outside the stage door smoking his cigarettes. He would always give me a wink and a smile. Though our views of working in Hollywood versus having to work outside of the business differed greatly when I became an adult, we're still friends and have been for many years.

But transitioning from working as an actress to working away from Hollywood is very difficult. I know this from firsthand experience. Being recognized can work both for and against you, and Paul and I do not always see eye to eye on this subject. Despite this, he has always been there for me when times were tough—and they were tough a lot later on, believe me.

Very often to save money on full set construction, one series at Screen Gems would "borrow" a standing set on another stage if a script called for one. One episode of Hazel featured a rock and roll band in which Bobby's character Harold Baxter was a member. The set required was a garage for the band to rehearse inside, and it just so happened on the particular day of shooting that scene, the garage set from The Donna Reed Show was available. So we all trucked over to that stage and used the garage for our show. I do remember meeting Donna Reed once or twice. She was nice but very consumed with her show because she was the co-executive producer, even though she never received screen credit for that. She didn't seem all that interested in young visitors, but she was always dressed so lovely with her perfectly-fitted dresses, pearls, and heels.

The Bewitched stage was across from the café. This was another one of my favorite stages to visit on my breaks. There was always this big, tall guard beside the stage door entrance to Bewitched, but he was friendly. He always had a warm greeting for Bobby and me. We would plead with him to let us go inside to watch when we weren't filming or in school on the lot. He always would look the other way, and we would sneak inside quietly and watch from the back of the stage, because we knew that if anyone saw us, we would be asked to leave. We also knew where to hide because their stage was set up similar to ours.

Just like the big guard, we knew too that some of the crew saw us, but they seemed to always look the other way as well. It was a real treat to see Endora (Agnes Moorehead) in her beautiful costumes of green, purple and chiffon, and that bright, red hair! We always got a kick out of it when she would raise her arms to cast a spell. That set was so much fun, because Bobby and I got to see them stop the action during the middle of a scene. The actors would all freeze on their marks while members of the crew jumped into the set, gave them props or took them away, or someone else would be placed in the set or taken out. Then they would resume filming. When the show aired, it really did look like magic taking place.

Elizabeth Montgomery was just radiant, and I loved watching her make those horrified and angry faces at her TV mother. I was surprised to see how tiny and petite she was in person. So were Donna Reed, Barbara Eden—and me, for that matter. I remember one time visiting the set during a break from Hazel that she was with her hairdresser, smoking a cigarette. I approached her and told her how beautiful I thought she was. She was quite shy, but she smiled back at me. Then she told me that I had better get back to my stage so the crew wouldn't worry about where I'd gone. Hmm, a little pensive, when I now look back on it.

On my way out to my own series, I noticed the latest addition to Bewitched in a far-off corner of the stage—the new baby that would come to be named Tabitha. It was wrapped in a blanket, however it was made of pink wax! It was a life-size doll that had stroke-like feathers all over it, obviously created by the Screen Gems prop department. It was really interesting, but kind of scary too! I remember as a kid I would always practice twitching my nose, hoping for something magical to happen. As much as I loved the Bewitched set, nothing compared to the Hazel set and Shirley Booth.

In the latter days of our series, I would occasionally see Sally Field as the soon-to-be "Flying Nun" running down the lot in her habit and full wardrobe with her makeup artist and costume designer racing alongside her. Her habit was almost as big as she was, and she was always so animated—laughing, giggling, talking, smiling and waving hello. We all knew each other on the lot, and just like when I practiced twitching my nose, I also wanted to fly like Sister Bertrille, so in my backyard, I'd jump from a very short tree and flap my arms like crazy on the quick trip down in an attempt to maybe get a little air. I never did.

When we arrived at Stage 5 for work on Hazel, our huge elephant door was open early in the morning, just like everyone else's. It was really cold inside while they blew out the morning air. The routine on Monday would be to first check in with the show's associate producer, then proceed to our dressing rooms with our shooting script for the week to unload our bags and wares. All the dressing room doors were open and being warmed up by the crew. In front of my dressing room was a director's chair. It was wooden, with yellow canvas for the seat part and white for the back, which also had my name stitched on both sides. How cool at eight years old to have my own director's chair!

On the very first day of production, my father had three dozen long-stemmed yellow and pink roses delivered to Stage 5 in a big, beautiful hand-painted vase. The card read, "Congratulations Julia! I'm so proud of you, Dad." For other days, we would meet at a big table in front of one of the main sets to have our first reading of the episode. Everyone was always happy to see one another. Besides our regular cast and perhaps a few actors who had been selected to play guest roles, also present would be our director, the writers, producers, and some of our key crew personnel.

The rest of the crew—the camera operator and his assistants, lighting men, sound engineers, grips, set designers, the guys who worked above us on the catwalks, the wardrobe and hair people, and everyone else who helped make our show the most professional it could be—would all be milling around the stage, doing their jobs and getting ready to shoot the show. Shirley was usually the last to arrive, and we all waited happily and patiently for her to join us. She always greeted us first before scurrying with her assistant into her own dressing room, which was right by the set.

I will always remember the very first Monday that we began production. That's because before we started reading the script that would set the premise for the season (the episode in which Hazel and Harold would come to live with my TV family), we all, as the new actors, went around the table introducing ourselves so the crew that had worked with Shirley the past four years could get to know us.

The script at the beginning of each week was always green in color. As changes were made during filming (for whatever reasons), we would get different colors for the affected pages to replace in our scripts. But for Monday readings, the pages were all green. We'd start on page one and remain completely in character until the last page. The director would set each scene as written and recite all the stage directions. It was very informal—we dressed casually and comfortably, and sometimes there would be wisecracks made as we plowed through the pages. Sometimes these readings would last two to three hours, so that the writers could determine what was working and what needed to be rewritten on those other colored pages.

After each reading, we'd take a break and then go to the set and start working on our blocking (staging and moving about while reading our lines aloud from our scripts). The director would position us, and our camera operator, Fred Gately, would observe and determine where his camera needed to be in order to get the coverage the director wanted. Incidentally, Fred was a Hollywood veteran whose career went back to the earliest days of television, working on Dragnet and Ozzie and Harriet when they were first getting started. He was also one of the sweetest men I've ever met. Everyone loved him. Frequently he would let me look through his camera lens while he was preparing to shoot.

After some initial blocking, we'd take a lunch break. Since Shirley was sometimes in every scene of every episode, the lunch break varied in time, depending on how much of it was needed for Shirley to prepare for the first scene to be filmed. So we'd either head to makeup and wardrobe and then back to our dressing rooms to go over lines while we ate if it was going to be a quick lunch, or we'd go to the little café or to the studio restaurant if we had at least an hour. Or if the break was going to be very long, Bobby and I would head to the school room for an hour or so of education before eating lunch.

The school room was a small but functional "room" built inside our soundstage for our studies with our teacher, Catherine Deeney. She was a wonderful woman, stern, but very funny. For some reason, she always keep an open bag of marshmallows in her desk drawer. They would dry out and were always stale, but we loved them.

From Tuesday through Friday, we would film the rest of the various scenes of each episode, and not necessarily in script order. If a show called for three scenes in the Baxter home at various places throughout the script, they were all filmed on the same day, since the set was already lit and all of the equipment was in place. If there were swing sets (like the garage I mentioned earlier), those were filmed on another day. If we needed to do any exterior shooting at the Ranch in Burbank, that would be on another day.

Throughout each day, we would film off and on, and when we weren't needed, we were completing the four hours of school that the state required us to have while we were working on the show. While the crew was lighting and setting up each shot in each scene, they would have little people stand-ins for us to take our positions so we could get our necessary school hours in and still get our scenes filmed on schedule.

Hazel was a one-camera show. This means that you do each scene several times so that the camera operator can capture different angles at different times. A master shot that encapsulates everyone in the scene would be shot first, then medium and two-shots of the various actors within the scene, and finally the close-ups of each actor. Afterward, Tom and the other film cutters worked from the director's notes and pieced all the different takes together to give each scene the variety it needed to keep the episode moving.

Each time the camera changes position, the set has to be relit so it is balanced with the previous takes. This can be quite time-consuming, so anytime minors are part of a scene, they are usually filmed first, and usually there's enough time during setups that they can be sent "back to school" to meet the minimum state education requirement. The child labor laws in California are such that a maximum of four hours per day is the limit for children working on a set as well. So it obviously makes good sense to bank both school time and work time, thus utilizing all eight hours to their utmost advantage.

However, very often Harold and Susie would only be in one or two scenes in the entire half hour, so once school was done for the day, and if our scenes were not going to be filmed right away, what did Bobby and Julia do? Why, we explored the Hollywood lot, the Ranch, visited the sets of other productions, and just had fun, fun, fun at Screen Gems! We were everywhere, until of course we were called back inside to work. Usually they knew where we were or they gave us a definite time to return.

So that was the routine for all twenty-nine episodes of Hazel during its fifth season on the air. It was a privilege and such a great gift that was given to me. In return, I gave them the talent I was blessed with, along with the discipline that had been instilled in me over my professional career.

FADE OUT

CHAPTER 3 - BEING SUSIE BAXTER

FADE IN: SCREEN GEMS STUDIOS, STAGE 5

I was very fortunate to be signed for all twenty-nine episodes of Hazel for the 1965-1966 season. There were several plots that featured Susie as the main subject, and I am truly grateful to the writers for having that much faith in me. To also be able to live my very young life at that time and be as close to Shirley Booth as I had become was truly an honor. She was a wonderful advisor on the Hollywood lifestyle (and what it meant to her). How blessed she said she was to have the career that she did. She truly was one of the industry's greatest actresses.

Shirley was the first to tell you that she wasn't the most beautiful woman or that perfect "size four" that Hollywood requires, but she honed her craft and was the recipient of so many accolades and awards from her peers and critics. She loved her work and had played opposite some of the best in movies, television and Broadway. I spent many, many hours alone with her in her dressing room during our breaks and lunches. I just loved to listen to her voice—so cute and different from anyone I'd ever worked with.

Her dressing room was always cold. That air conditioner was always on! There was a bed/couch on one side of the room and a dressing studio mirror on the other with a nice leather white chair. Shirley always relaxed in her slip, and her various wigs were on the stand by the light-up mirror. She loved all kinds of raw nuts and dried fruit. Shirley had a private phone with several lines that allowed her to talk to many people at once, and she could call anywhere in the world. That may not sound like a big deal today, but remember that this was 1965.

Not once did she ever ask me to leave, not even during a phone call or when she would dress for an upcoming scene. She never once refused to let me come in and visit—her door was always open to me. We spoke of so many subjects, including our personal lives.

Shirley loved to drive the cars the network would buy brand new for her each year. She loved her home. While she loved her role as the busybody maid running everyone's life, Shirley always told me that she also listened to the people in charge that helped guide her to make the right decision to do the series. She told me that was the secret to success in Hollywood. We talked endlessly, we laughed, and she loved all of my stuffed animals and drawings. Sometimes she would start a story and we would finish it together, not necessarily on paper, but just talking and creating a magical picture of fantasy and imagination for fun!

One time Shirley asked me if everyone was treating me nicely—not just on our stage, but on the entire lot. Well, everyone was nice, except for the one time Bobby and I went over to the stage where they were filming the Jerry Lewis movie *Three on a Couch*. There's a scene in the film that involves a golf cart that's literally up in the air in front of a huge backdrop. Bobby and I went to that set on the day it was being filmed, and Jerry (who was also directing) spotted us at the very back of the stage. He looked right in our direction and yelled, "Get those fucking kids off my set!" Bobby, who was not afraid of anyone or anything, yelled back, "Why? We just want to watch!" Jerry would have no part of it. "Out, out, out! Get the fuck out now, you little bastards!" Bobby, up for the challenge, retorted, "I've been on this lot longer than you! We don't need to watch your stupid scene anyway. Come on, let's go!" Jerry gave us another "Out!" and then Bobby—and I was so proud of him—yelled back at Jerry, "Go to hell!" Needless to say, we left.

Once outside, we laughed so hard and promised never to tell anyone about it. I never did tell Shirley, but Bobby was right about one thing—he had been at Columbia longer than Jerry Lewis had been at the time. It was always like that with Bobby, never a dull moment. We were literally like two peas in a pod. We did everything together on and off the set. We never did socialize much with any of the other kids on the lot; we were too busy having fun by ourselves.

While one star on the lot could be mean and nasty to kids, another could be an absolute sweetheart. Right next door in the adjacent soundstage to *Hazel* on one occasion, the legendary Cary Grant was doing pick-ups for what would turn out to be his last film, *Walk, Don't Run*. Bobby wanted me to meet him (he previously had the honor). Once again, we had a guard to get past, one who was specifically told not to allow anyone but cast and crew inside. But when had that ever stopped us before? After all, we had already been called "little bastards" by Jerry Lewis, so we were fearless by this point.

It helped a little that Bobby knew the guard this time, but the guard explained that he would be in trouble if he let us inside. But Bobby wouldn't take no for an answer. He pled with the guard for about ten minutes, showing him his baseball cards and telling the guard how much he knew Cary would love to see this one collector's card he had just bought. Finally, the guard caved. He said he would turn and walk behind the stage door for fifteen seconds, and if anyone asked him, he would state that he never saw anyone go inside. So, in we went.

Mr. Grant was rehearsing a scene where it looked like he was trying to climb up a wall and there was a catwalk-type scaffolding under him. The backdrop was all white, and he was dressed in a very handsome suit. He noticed Bobby. "Hello Bobby, how are you doing?" he asked. Bobby asked him how he was, and they exchanged pleasantries for a bit until Mr. Grant asked who his friend was. Bobby said, "I'd like you to meet my co-star, Julia Benjamin." "You have very good taste in women," was Mr. Grant's response.

Then he turned to me and said, "Hello Julia, nice to meet you, and thank you for coming and visiting me today." Bobby told Mr. Grant he had a new baseball card to show him (what he told the guard was absolutely legitimate - baseball was BIG in 1965). Mr. Grant explained that he was hung up at the moment (literally), but "After I get down from here, I would love to see that card." True to his word, after they shot the scene, he came over to us, kissed my hand, he and Bobby talked about the card, and then we left. We passed the guard on the way out. He didn't even look at us, but Bobby said goodbye to him, and he told us to have a nice day. As we walked back to our stage, Bobby made me promise not to tell anyone where we went, and I didn't.

So later that week, Catherine (my teacher), my mom and I were leaving our stage for the day. At that precise moment, Mr. Grant was leaving his stage, carrying a briefcase and walking with his assistant. We all approached each other, and I ran over to Mr. Grant and said, "Hi, Cary. Are you going home too?" My mom at first couldn't believe what she was seeing, then scolded me for not calling him Mr. Grant. He said, "Well, hello Julia, honey." Then he said to my mom, "She *should* call me Cary because we're old famous friends."

Well, that of course stopped my mom and Catherine dead in their tracks. Their mouths were both wide open. He continued, "Hello ladies. It's always a pleasure to see Julia." Then he took the red rose from his lapel, handed it to me and said, "Beautiful little ladies must have beautiful flowers, and you, Julia, will be and are a beautiful little lady." Then he kissed my hand. We said our goodbyes, and he told me to say hello to Bobby.

My mom and Catherine didn't say a word as we walked to our cars. Not one word. They were speechless! I did notice that both of them were blushing bright red, were a bit flustered and were giggling a little. They were most likely getting ready to discipline me for approaching such a big star and being so forward with him, but that scenario luckily went out the window very quickly. Needless to say, it was a very fun ride home. Mom put the radio on, and we sang and laughed all the way back to the valley. Cary was such a nice man. He was so handsome—and he smelled really good too!

Bobby and I always had so much fun on the lot. The mid 1960s was the era of scooters and motorbikes. Bobby built a homemade motorbike and brought it to the studio, hidden in the back of his mom's station wagon. He said he used to put it in the back of the car and cover it up with a blanket at night while she was making dinner so she didn't know it was there when they left each morning. He also told me that he had a key to the car that nobody ever knew about too.

So one day, he took it out on one of our breaks. It truly was homemade—it had a wooden seat, long red handlebars and a real gas engine, just like a scooter and bicycle combined. He rolled it over to where the transportation vehicles for the studio were parked behind our stage. He had me be the lookout—he wanted me to warn him if our mothers or anyone else might be coming near.

Then he pulled out a long tube from his pocket, put one end in his mouth and the other end into the gas tank of one of the transportation vehicles. He started sucking until the gas came out, and he put it into the tank of his motorbike until it was full and we could ride it around the lot. This went on for days. He siphoned, I looked out, until we eventually got caught by the transportation supervisor. He didn't say a word to us, nor we to him. Bobby just calmly took the tube, put it in his pocket and looked at me. I got on the back of the bike and we left the scene of the crime, again laughing all the way and promising not to tell anyone.

One time my TV mom, Lynn Borden, caught us. Bobby dropped everything, ran over to Lynn and calmly said, "Hi." Lynn figured it out, laughed and muttered, "You kids!" and walked away. She didn't tattle on us, so we got away with it again. Ah, but this was just the beginning of our Screen Gems antics.

When we were shooting the opening credits for the show outside the Baxter home at the Ranch (where the exterior shots for the fronts of all the Screen Gems series homes were located), we wandered around during a break and discovered a set that was dressed for some kind of a shoot that involved giant, gray petrified rocks. We picked them up—they were practically weightless—and threw them at each other.

Another time, there was a man-made pond with all these wooden canoes alongside of it. Even though we were in our wardrobe for whatever we were going to soon shoot, we had plenty of time. So we dragged one of the canoes over to the water and got in it. What we didn't know is that it had half-inch holes that had been drilled out of the bottom. Once we discovered this, we wanted to see if we could make it to the other side of the pond before our shoes got wet. Unfortunately, right before we made land, our moms discovered us. Boy, were they mad! They started screaming at us, and Bobby yelled back, "We're not wet! Hold on, we'll get out!"

We did get out, luckily far away from our parents on the other side of the pond. Both of us made a beeline back to the stage, way out-distancing our military moms, and once again laughing all the way. By the time our mothers got back, they were out of breath and luckily too tired to do anything to us. Instead, they sat down and had a smoke together. Our moms were just like kids too, sharing their packs of cigs and even Shirley would occasionally come over and ask them for a smoke.

There was also fun with a baseball. We were filming on a swing set inside one of the stages at the Ranch, and it was taking forever. It seemed liked hours. They didn't need us right away, so we went outside and played our version of bowling first. That soon led to playing catch, and then Bobby noticed the building. "Look!" he said.

We both glanced at the very top of the soundstage. Each stage is numbered. That number is usually at the corner of the building. Well, next to this stage number, the corner of the building was literally starting to crumble. So we did the obvious thing two kids with a baseball would do when presented with this opportunity—we took turns to see if we could help the building crumble faster.

Bobby went first, to show me what to do, and I followed his lead. Now, remember that they were shooting our show inside while we were doing this. First Harold Lewis, our wonderful associate producer, came out and asked, "What are you kids doing?" "Nothing," we said. He went back inside. We waited a few minutes and started to throw the ball again. The building crumbles more.

Next came out one of the audio engineers. "What are you kids doing?" "Nothing." He looked up at the sky and then went back inside. We heard him yell, "No planes. What the hell *is* that?" Again, the building demolition kids continued their mission. We turned around a few moments later and there's Bobby's mother Maxine, who just witnessed everything. "Give it to me right now!" The ball was confiscated, and our baseball game was called on account of parenthood.

One of the reasons we had so much time between our scenes was because Ray Fulmer, who played my dad, developed a terrible stuttering problem. Sometimes it hours and around fifty to seventy takes to get scenes shot with him. Other times it felt like they always waited until the seventh hour of our eight-hour day to shoot our scenes. That meant we always had a lot of time to play after our school hours were done.

Now, no one ever yelled or screamed at Ray, though those retakes sure took their toll on Shirley. She was absolutely exhausted by the end of some of those days. But Catherine Denney (our teacher/welfare worker) was very strict when it came to the end of the day cutoff time for us. Frequently she would stand at the edge of the set, glancing down at her watch and making sure everyone from our director that week to the actors to the crew knew that it was time for Julia and Bobby to go home. We really loved Catherine. She was the best studio teacher anyone could ask for, and she became such good friends with both of our moms.

One day when we were shooting at the Ranch, we didn't know where our mothers were. Everyone was looking for them. We eventually discovered they had climbed up the tree across the street from the facade of our *Hazel* house. There they were, sitting on a big branch, smoking like two kids who had just been caught doing a no-no in a hiding place. But they were quietly laughing. Bobby and I looked at each other and then yelled at them, "And you think *we're* the bad ones?! Your grown-ups! You should know better!"

It turned out that while they were able to get up there by themselves, they needed help getting down. Even Shirley got a big kick out of it. "I think I'll come up there and join you gals," she joked. But then Harold Lewis, our always-concerned-about-everything associate producer, said, "Shirley, no! Please! I have the kids, the crew and the rest of the cast. Are you people all trying to give me a heart attack?!"

Harold was a worrier (all associate producers are hired and paid to do just that), but he was a great guy. Sometimes he would drive my mom and me to the Brown Derby for lunch. We all sat in one of the big booths that were in the front of the restaurant. I remember seeing Lucille Ball there one day, and I wanted so much to go and introduce myself to her, not knowing then that I would work with her and Henry Fonda in the film *Yours, Mine and Ours* about a year after *Hazel* wrapped (I was one of the children singing the theme for the opening titles). But my mother would not let me leave the table.

At one point, Harold excused himself and said he'd be right back. We were just about to finish our lunch when all of a sudden Lucy herself walked up to our table and asked me, "Are you Julia?" Of course I responded that I was, and she said, "I just loved your performance on *Valentine's Day*. You were terrific!" My mom's mouth dropped to the floor. Then Lucy leaned over in my mom's direction and said, "Toni, Julia can come and say hi to me anytime, and say hi to Phil for me too, dear." It turned out that Lucy also knew my dad personally!

As a matter of fact—and I don't think this has ever been published anywhere before—on *I Love Lucy*, when Ricky is discovered by a talent scout prior to the Ricardos leaving for Hollywood, the scout's name is Mr. Benjamin. Lucy had told the writers to call him that because of her friendship with my dad (they for some reason changed his first name on the show, though). Anyway, my mother told her it was an honor to meet her and how much she and I both loved her work. Harold came back to the table to pay the bill, and we knew what he had just done! He picked me up and carried me out of the Brown Derby, and we drove back to Columbia. Harold loved to carry me around the set with him, especially in the morning when I would first arrive. I just adored him.

One week we began shooting in the morning, and the audio engineer was very frustrated because there was a noise coming from somewhere. They had to keep stopping the filming. It was a light sawing type of sound. After the third time, they finally found the source of the disturbance. There was a woman on the stage in a chair next to the big table where we would have our readings. She was filing her fingernails! She'd stop and look around every time the director would yell "Cut!" and started up again as soon as he yelled "Action!" It was Harold's job to go the woman and tell her to stop. It turned out that neither he nor anyone else on the stage knew who she was. We had no guest actors scheduled for that day, and she wasn't a friend or relative of anyone there! She simply got up and left, and probably went to another soundstage to continue her manicure.

I loved shooting the episodes that were written just for me, especially the ones that had Susie's black cat in the scenes. The animal trainer would bring in five black cats every time there was a scene that called for the cat. All five looked exactly the same, but they were all different sizes and weights. One cat was very light. This cat was used when I would have to carry the kitty with me. There was a slightly larger black cat for the scenes in which the cat was sitting next to me, and a third one was used if it called for the cat to walk near or follow me. The other two were "backup cats" in case something went wrong with the other three. Nothing like being prepared. Needless to say, I loved all five of them very much.

There's one episode where I played "dress up" in my TV mom's pale green chiffon dress. I was in a wheel barrel making mud pies! This is one of my favorite episodes. I remember the wardrobe lady putting the gown right over my regular clothes. I also remember Harold Lewis picking me up and putting me in the wheel barrel before the filming started. The animal trainer brought the bigger black cat into the scene to lay down in the barrel beside me. The director that week told me to have as much fun with the mud as I wanted, so naturally the black cat and I got *really* dirty! However, when they put the water in to make the mud, the cat didn't like this one bit and immediately leaped out of the barrel during the shot. So the trainer had to bring in one of the backup cats (who didn't mind the mud) to finish the scene. Wonder if the two backup cats flipped a coin to see who would be the stunt double for the prima donna big cat?

In another show, I had a kitchen scene with Shirley where I was trying to climb up on the counter to get something out of the cupboard while holding the lighter black cat. Honestly, this animal would simply dangle over my arm, just like a rag doll, not fuss or even try to get away—what a pro!

For every one of these scenes that involved any one of my black kitties, the trainer was always right on the edge of the set to take them immediately once a shot was concluded. The cats would always be on the set an hour or so before we needed them in the scene. I wanted so to play with them before we started and pet them between takes, but the trainer explained to me that his animals were working actors just like I was. They had to stay in their travel cages at all times when they weren't performing. He really treated them like they were his babies. He didn't want them to run off or get hurt. He pointed up to the catwalks where our grips climbed to light the scenes and said, "Look, Julia, the catwalk is thirty feet up, and if the cats took that name literally and dashed up there, it would be very difficult to get them down." I completely understood. He really did care for those animals—they always looked so shiny. Their fur was sleek and jet black. They were all so beautifully groomed, had such sweet spirit, and were so well-trained and talented.

In another episode, Susie started taking ballet classes. One scene took place in the Baxter living room and besides myself, it included all of the principal actors—Shirley, Ray, Lynn and Bobby. Our director that week was Bill Russell, who was kind of a stern gentleman. I had on black tights and a leotard with accompanying black ballet slippers, and I remember how badly I wanted to wear this brand new red tutu costume from Capezio's that the wardrobe lady had purchased for me. The outfit was so frilly, and it really was just the most perfect costume I had ever seen. Any eight-year-old girl would literally be in heaven when she put it on. Mr. Russell nixed the idea because he felt it looked way too advanced for someone taking her first ballet lesson.

Well, it probably was, but the wardrobe lady tried to talk him into allowing it. "Nope, sorry," was the response she got. I was really upset. Shirley saw this and went over to him herself. "Bill, Julia has already seen the costume. I think it would be a good idea if she could just go ahead and wear it. This is one of her moments." Then, before he could give her an answer, Shirley gave me a wink, turned to the crew and quickly announced, "Let's get this shot done, kids! I have a lunch date today!"

Well, that's all it took! Mr. Russell called me over, told me to go ahead and put on the costume and then get prepared to shoot the scene. I was so happy! I remember only doing that scene twice—one to print and one for protection. I already knew how to dance because my parents put me in ballet and tap classes when I was three. When the scene was finished, everyone on the stage applauded. They remarked that not only was I a natural, but they commented on how delicately and beautifully I used my hands.

Truth be told, I actually created that dance myself. When the writers came up with the idea for the script, they had approached me to find out if I could indeed dance and if I could show them a sample of what I could do. I assume now looking back that they needed to make sure I could really dance before they went to the trouble of writing that episode. So I did an impromptu performance and danced my way into their hearts right there on the spot. They were satisfied, told me "Thank you," kissed my hand and retreated to their offices to brainstorm. Oh, and Shirley did indeed make her lunch date after we finished filming the scene.

There was another episode when we all went camping. A lot of this episode was shot outside at the Ranch in Burbank, and it was HOT! The San Fernando Valley is known for its intensely hot summers. It was well over one hundred degrees that week, and the camping episode was taking place in the winter! We all had to dress in flannels, long sleeve shirts, jeans, and coats. Why was it that winter scenes in television shows back then seemed to always be filmed in the summer and vice versa?

Of course our trailer dressing rooms were all air conditioned, but when I stepped outside in full wardrobe, it was so hot that after several minutes, I began to faint. Harold Lewis saw this, quickly grabbed me and put me back in my dressing room. Shirley decided that we should wait for the sun to die down a little—it was early in the afternoon—and we would resume shooting a couple of hours later. Some of us remained in our trailers until we absolutely had to go outside. Tarps were set up for us to stay under next to the set when we did go out. They helped a little bit. Bobby didn't seem to mind the heat as much as I did. He actually went riding around the Ranch on his motorbike until he was asked to stop because of the heat.

A decision was made to shoot everything they could with the adult actors and then bring Bobby and I onto the set after everything else was filmed. I remember Ray waiting outside to shoot one part of the scene. It was taking so long that he went ahead and removed all of his wardrobe, remaining in his own summer clothing until just before the camera would roll. I don't recall Lynn being bothered too much by the heat, but I was inside my trailer for most of their filming.

Shirley came to my dressing room, concerned about what had happened to me earlier, and asked if I just wanted to go home and postpone the filming until the weather cooled off. I assured her that I was there to work and I'd be alright. She said, "Julia, you and

Bobby are two of the finest child actors that I have ever worked with—you two are real troupers!" And with that, she opened the door from my trailer to go outside, stuck her arm out and felt the blistering heat, turned back to me and exclaimed, "Boy, it's a real doozy out there!" Talk about jumping back into character! But it was exactly how we all felt.

Whenever food was used in a scene, Hoppy, one of our property masters, would always be the person in charge of it on the set. On this afternoon, he stopped by my trailer with cold drinks, fruit, and a big snow cone for me. He was just the best! Hoppy did all the cooking of the food too. His "headquarters" was at the back of Stage 5 at Screen Gems in Hollywood. He had a couple of burners on a table, and all of the food was stored in a refrigerator and on shelving above it. Visitors to our set always smelled something quite yummy being prepared when they entered our soundstage. No one was ever allowed over to his domain, though. If anyone ever did, he'd take a towel, snap it at you, and snarl to stay away. It was all in fun, but he really was serious and we respected his wishes, if nothing else but for health and safety reasons.

Speaking of Hoppy, in another episode, there was a dinner scene back on Stage Five at Screen Gems. We were all having asparagus with hollandaise sauce. Once again, it was the entire regular cast—Shirley, Ray, Lynn, Bobby, and me. The scene seemed like it was taking hours to shoot because of Ray's stuttering problem. As I said, nobody ever yelled at Ray; they were always patient with him. But at one point, Bobby had just about had enough and exclaimed, "Come on, Ray, it's only one sentence!" We were all so bored and exhausted from shooting and re-shooting.

At about take thirty, Hoppy, in charge of placing the food on the set, started yelling at Bobby and me because we were devouring his asparagus with each take, and he had to keep making more and more. "But I'm hungry, Hoppy," Bobby kept saying. "We've been sitting here for hours." Bobby and I both started laughing, and then Hoppy and Bobby playfully started bickering back and forth. At least it broke up some of the monotony.

We literally got to take fifty, and still there was nothing that could be printed. Shirley was growing weary. The director could sense this and told our camera operator Fred Gately to reposition the camera and shoot at a different angle—from Hazel's point of view—so Shirley could go back to her dressing room. They took a break so the director of photography and the grips could re-light the set, but we all had to stay. Eventually we got the shot. Needless to say, Bobby and I also had our fill of asparagus with hollandaise sauce for quite a while.

We had a breakfast scene in another episode that also took some time to shoot. Cornflakes was Hoppy's food of the day for us on this occasion. Bobby and I ate three full bowls. Once again, Hoppy was hopping mad at us for consuming all of his props. But what Hoppy didn't know this time was that after those three bowls, Bobby would finish his next bowl, then go under the table, give me that empty bowl, take my full bowl, and then go back to his chair from under the table. Everyone but Hoppy knew what was happening. At one point, Hoppy looked over at our moms and asked, "Don't you two ever feed these children?!" We and the crew all laughed, and eventually Hoppy figured it out. Bobby told Hoppy that he ate all the cereal so he could finish the scene and go look at his baseball cards and ride his motorbike.

Shirley and Bobby were very close. What was so great about that was that whenever Bobby would pull a gag or a prank on the set, Shirley would go right along with it. Eventually I was part of that fun too. Sometimes it felt like she was just one big kid. We had so much fun.

This is not to say that Bobby and I always got along. Like typical kids, for one reason or another, we had our share of disagreements and spats. One day on Stage Five, we got mad at each other. Bobby started teasing me, and I yelled back at him. This did not resolve itself by the time we both had to go to school. While we were in the schoolroom, our teacher Catherine walked out, and once she was gone, Bobby locked me inside. I was furious and started screaming. They were shooting on the set. Everyone heard me yelling to Bobby to open the door and let me out. The door had a latch that could only be opened with a steel lock key, and Catherine had that key. She was nowhere to be found.

They stopped filming—I had ruined the shot. The whole crew came running back to the schoolroom. Catherine apparently had gone to the ladies' room and nobody knew it. She could not be found. It was only for about five minutes, but it felt like five hours. When Catherine finally came back and unlocked the door, Bobby looked at me and snapped, "And I'll do it again, too!"

And he did, in other ways. There were times when he'd take Petunia (my stuffed bulldog) and hold it high above my head so I couldn't reach it, take my pencils away from me when Catherine wasn't looking, make marks on my schoolwork and ruin my homework, just about anything he could think of.

Fortunately, the good times were more frequent than the bad. Deep down we were friends and really cared about each other. We never tattled on one another, we had each other's back, and there were so many times that Shirley joined in on our fun, especially when we all had to be so patient with Ray during some grueling takes and retakes.

Shirley was amazing. She took an interest in Bobby's baseball cards, and they actually talked baseball a lot during those times between takes when we couldn't leave the set. Shirley used to make these animated, cartoon-like voices while we were playing. She'd make the entire crew roar and laugh so hard that we'd all have to take a break to literally compose ourselves.

She could contort her face like nobody I'd ever seen before. It was hilarious. She would burst into "I'm a little teapot short and stout," then look at Bobby and say, "Come on, Sport, give me a beat!" Bobby would start using whatever utensils were near him on the set to play the drums, and I'd start clapping along. Lynn would be pretending to dance while sitting in her chair, and Ray would say, "Yeah, man!" It was so funny that the whole crew would stop what they were doing just to watch Shirley.

Sometimes the crew would start dancing and skipping along with us while they were lighting the set, putting the props in place, rolling the boom microphone into the set, etc. Frequently, they would sing along with us while they were working. Just picture these guys, big, tall, rugged Teamsters all singing the teapot song and jumping around! So even when it was a difficult day, Shirley always found a way to make it fun. Every single day with her was an absolute joy.

There was an episode in which Bobby and I were at the top of the stairs inside our house. When the director yelled "Action!" Bobby took my hand, and we started running down the long flight of stairs, but I missed a step and he ended up dragging me down most of the way. I was bumping and stumbling over each step, and he didn't know it. By the time I reached the bottom, our associate producer Harold Lewis was already down on one knee ready to catch me before I hit the studio floor, and he did, of course.

Part of the problem was that my real house didn't have any stairs, but Bobby's did. So not only was I not used to stairs, but they were a bit overwhelming too. Harold asked me if I was OK. I was a little scuffed and bruised, but otherwise just fine. Everyone started yelling at Bobby. I told them that I was OK, just not used to racing down stairs. Bobby *really* didn't know I had fallen behind him. I assured him that I was fine and told everyone not to yell at him.

Bobby was clearly upset over what had just transpired and said to me, "Don't you know how to go down stairs? Jeez, girls!" We took a break. Bobby and I walked around together, and he asked me again if I was alright. This time I could sense that he really felt bad. We'd had our spats, but I knew he was sincere. I told him I was OK. Remember that I was eight and Bobby was thirteen. Five years' difference when you're a kid is a lot more than five years when you're an adult. Even though we were both small for our respective ages, there was a big difference in maturity. We'd have our childish disagreements, there was a lot of teasing like that locked door incident and a few others, but Bobby never meant to seriously hurt me physically or emotionally in any way, and this was definitely the closest thing to that actually happening.

For the most part, Bobby was more like an older brother to me than a co-worker. In fact, right at the beginning of the season, Bobby was always there to make sure I hit my mark and know my cues, even if he wasn't in the shot. Many times I would wait off screen to make an entrance, and Bobby would wait there with me, just to make sure. Our teacher/welfare worker Catherine would always supervise us too. She used to tell Bobby to eat his tomatoes at lunch when we would all eat together at the studio restaurant outside the main entrance to Columbia. Bobby just hated tomatoes, so when Catherine insisted, he would gag on them, barely swallow them, and then complain to everyone at the table that he should not be forced to eat something that he did not like. So he was just a typical boy that for the most part looked out for his "little sister."

Around the middle of the season, my two front baby teeth started getting loose. For continuity reasons (in case they wanted to air shows out of shooting order), the producers asked that my two front teeth plus the two baby teeth along each side of them be pulled. They would then fit me with a plate that had four front fake teeth on it to wear until my permanent ones had grown in. Believe it or not, I didn't mind what they wanted to do so much as I did having to go to the dentist. I hated going to the dentist, and I only wore the plate during shooting, when I had to do so.

So one day my mom and Bobby's mom, Maxine, went out to lunch together during our break. They were going to go with our wardrobe mistress to a local department store to buy more clothes for us to wear on the show. But the wardrobe lady wasn't feeling well, so our moms went there by themselves. Bobby and I stayed on the set together and had lunch in the small café. We finished early and went back to Stage Five. It was totally empty—the crew was still at lunch. But Shirley was in her dressing room taking a nap. Bobby and I decided to climb up on the catwalk, since we had nobody stopping us.

When we got up top, we sat up there for quite a while and remained totally silent while we watched the crew return from lunch. While it was really cool being up there, we knew we had to be careful coming down so nobody would spot us. We made it down safely and decided to play with an old wicker wheelchair we found in the corner of the stage. It creaked and rattled so loudly that it woke Shirley up. She opened up her dressing room just enough so we could hear her say, "Sport, you and Julia tell those kids making all that noise that Shirley is taking a nap. Please ask them to go play somewhere else." Bobby said, "OK, Shirl. We will." I never found whether Shirley knew it was us all the time and was just being nice about it or whether she really thought there were other kids fooling around. It was yet another example of how wonderful this lady was.

But it didn't matter. There was no more time to play because by now, they were ready to shoot the next scene, which involved Bobby and me. So we started to shoot, and right in the middle of our scene, Bobby exclaimed, "Hey! Julia doesn't have her teeth in!" So they stopped the filming. Everyone started laughing, and I was so embarrassed. We had to wait until our moms came back, because my mom had the plate in her purse. Bobby, as my "older brother," then nicely told me that I needed to keep my "stuff" with me at all times—my plate, my inhaler for my asthma, and whatever else—because we shouldn't have to depend on anyone but ourselves and had to act grown-up when working in Hollywood. You know what? He was right.

Bobby was always guiding me and looking out for my best interests. We used to run to the Bank of America on Fridays when we got our paychecks, and our mothers were always running after us close behind. Bobby would grab my hand, and we always jaywalked across the street in busy Hollywood on Gower and Sunset to get to the bank.

Bobby's family had a poodle that had puppies during our season on *Hazel*. My mom and I picked out one of the puppies, which we named Susie. She was a great dog. Susie loved to jump off the diving board at our house and was such a great companion to our whole family.

Before the season ended, Bobby had a birthday party at his house. We played "Spin the Bottle." You know how that game goes—the person spinning and the eventual target of the bottle would have to go into the closet and kiss. Bobby spun, and you can guess that it landed on me. Now it can be told: Bobby was my first kiss. Well, I knew by that kiss that Bobby really did like me, and I liked him back. We were such good friends, and we shared so much of our (and our families') lives together at that studio. We could really talk to each other about being child stars and just growing up in general. Honestly, he really was a very down-to-earth boy, and hey, I was a pretty down-to-earth girl, too.

So many child stars have had bad experiences during their working years. It makes me sad thinking about them. I can honestly only remember two times in my entire acting career in which I have unpleasant memories. Both were during the season I was co-starring on *Hazel*.

One of our directors was a gentleman named E.W. Swackhamer. He was part of that rotating unit of directors at Screen Gems that made the rounds of all the sitcoms filming there at the time. The first week he was assigned to our show, I found him to be quite bullying and downright mean. Whether he took an instant disliking to me or didn't enjoy working with young actors, I can't say for sure, but it was starting out to be a very difficult week for me, and I was not happy.

My mom and dad went out one night early in that week, and when they returned, I was still awake. Clearly they sensed something was wrong, and they asked me about it. I told them that Swackhamer was being mean to me and that I didn't want to work with him. I remember both of my parents sitting with me for quite a while, listening attentively. My dad calmly assured me it would all be OK, and after hearing that, I was able to finally fall asleep.

The next day, my dad, whose office was stationed at Fox, left his studio and came over to Columbia, much to my surprise. In front of the whole crew, he pulled Swackhamer aside and asked him what his problem was. "Did she forget her lines? Is she not behaving like a professional?" he said. Swackhamer denied there was any issue, and after some discussion which I could not make out, I heard my dad say to him, "So it's *me* you don't like, not my daughter? If you've got a beef, take it out on *me*, not Julia." To this day, I still don't know what that "beef" was, but boy, Swackhamer sure changed his attitude toward me after that. He was much nicer to work with from that point on.

The other bad time stemmed from a recurring actress on the show whose name was Mala Powers. She was a close friend of Lynn Borden's in real life, and they cast her on the show as Barbara's friend, Mona. Mala was a prima donna. She had done some movies and some episodic television. Although certainly not a household name, she had a list of credits, but she also had a real "hoity toity" attitude about herself that rubbed me the wrong way. She was not a nice person.

Now, we as the regular cast members got the nicer dressing rooms. Guest and recurring actors got the smaller rooms, and sometimes they were relegated to large transportation trucks that housed four or five very small rooms together on one big flatbed cab. I assume this was the case for Mala whenever she was playing Mona on our show. One day, she had some woman coming to the set to interview her and decided to park her carcass in *my* dressing room to do the interview, because obviously what the show had given her was not good enough for her to entertain this reporter.

So I walked in, and there she is. She had made herself quite comfortable and had the nerve to tell me to leave because she was busy with this interview. She said she would be done in fifteen minutes. I politely responded, "Please leave my dressing room now. First, it's not yours. Second, my mom is not feeling well. She needs to rest." As Mala got up to leave, she told me in front of my mother that I needed to learn some manners. Fortunately, my mother had heard the whole thing and pretty much felt the same way about Mala as I did.

I remember telling Bobby later what had happened. "Oh, she's a real bitch!" he said. "I don't like her either, because she's always talking down to me. I've done more work than she has." Bobby was so cool—worked at Columbia longer than Jerry Lewis and acted in more shows than Mala Powers. You gotta love him.

Outside of Mala, we had no other prima donnas on *Hazel*. Everyone was always professional and incredibly kind. Corny as it sounds, we were indeed a family, and that was because of Shirley. Our set was always clean, everybody was happy and grateful for the work, and there was genuine care and concern for one another, right down to each and every member of our crew. Everyone there was just as important as the next person.

At Christmas time, Shirley came to my dressing room and handed me a beautiful velvet box. Inside was a solid gold medallion with the Patron Saint of the Theater, St. Genesis, Guide My Career, in the center of it, along with the actors' mask symbols (comedy and drama), with stars all around and curtains in the background. I'm pretty sure Shirley had this made just for me, so it's one-of-a-kind, and the inscription on the back reads, "To Julia, Love, Shirley Booth 12-24-65." It's almost too heavy to wear, but I do to this very day.

Christmas on our set was unbelievable. My mom bought a present for each and every person on our crew, beautifully wrapped boxes from the department store in gold and red with ribbons around them. I was so happy because I got to give everyone the beautiful presents and wish them all a very merry Christmas. The crew was genuinely touched—all these big men had tears in their eyes! I got a lot of presents too. That year our home had so many presents. Under our Christmas tree, it was so crowded that a lot of presents for my dad had to be leaned up against the wall in our living room. It truly was a holiday to remember.

Shortly after the New Year, our happiness turned to sadness when we found out that we were not going to be picked up for another season. It wasn't a question of ratings. Even though the show was not doing as well after *The Andy Griffith Show* as CBS had hoped, the network was willing to renew us. But Shirley was having health issues. She was approaching seventy years old, and the work schedule was taking its toll.

I can't say for sure, but Ray's stuttering problem was most likely a factor in her decision. Although by this point we were all used to his scenes taking much longer to complete, Ray seemed to develop a cavalier attitude about the whole thing and wasn't as guilt-ridden nor as apologetic as he was when it started to become a serious problem. He was not even attempting to do anything about it. It was business as usual for him. Nevertheless, Shirley never once complained.

After my mom and I heard the news about the cancellation, upset doesn't begin to describe the way we felt. When Shirley came into my dressing room after we filmed the last scene for the last episode, she found us both crying our eyes out. This was our family, and knowing we were not coming back was absolutely heartbreaking after what had become the greatest year of my short life.

Shirley sat down right next to me and said, "Julia, God never closes a door that he doesn't open a window." Somehow that calmed me. I stopped crying. We all chatted, even laughed at times. Then we all hugged. Shirley left my dressing room, said goodbye to everyone and walked out of the soundstage to her waiting car, which was just outside the big elephant door. She waved one last time, blew kisses, got in her car and drove off the lot. It was like the end of a big budget movie, like Mary Poppins flying away to her next adventure.

A while after the show ended, I was staying with Lynn Borden at her home for a few days. We both had to go to the unemployment office (as all actors do when they are not working). When we got there, we were surprised to discover both Ray and Bobby in line! Honestly, Bobby had grown so tall since I had last seen him. He wasn't a boy anymore, he was a man—a very handsome man. I mean, he was really big. We didn't say a word to each other. He simply made a gesture as to how small I still was and how he no longer was. Yeah, that was the extent of our reunion. It was strange, but you know what? All the time we had spent that year on *Hazel* really did speak for itself.

One thing that did occur was so many people recognized all of us. They asked for our autographs and if they could take pictures with us. Of course we obliged. Ray left, and then so did Bobby. That encounter at the unemployment office was the last time I saw him.

Shortly afterward, Bobby and his family left Hollywood. He had a sister named Stella, and she was having a lot of problems. Bobby and I could relate quite well to each other because we were having similar issues with my sister, Betty. Bobby and I would sometimes talk about what was going on at our homes and how much grief it was causing our parents. We felt bad because here we were laughing and enjoying ourselves while we were working, but our parents were suffering both emotionally and financially trying to deal with our sisters.

Eventually, Bobby's mother Maxine decided that Hollywood was contributing to Stella's problems, so the Buntrock family moved to South Dakota. Rumor has it that Bobby joined the National Guard while there. Maxine died in 1972, apparently from cardiac arrest at their home in Keystone. Two years later, Bobby died in a terrible car accident on a bridge near their home, and then rumors starting flying around that his mother had not died from cardiac arrest at their home as originally had been reported, but from a fatal car accident on that same bridge two years earlier. Whatever actually did happen to both Maxine and to Bobby, the truth of the matter is that two warm, wonderful people left us way too soon.

My TV mom, Lynn Borden, passed away in February of 2015. This hit me particularly hard because of my affection for her not just as an actress, but also as a human being. We kept in touch over the years, and she always lent a kind and generous ear to whatever was going on in my life. I've had my ups and downs financially, and once when I was really down and out, she invited my son Branden and I to move in until I got back on my feet. Although I never took her up on that, it has remained as one of the most noble, generous gestures anyone has ever given me.

During the last few years of her life, Lynn never told me that her doctor discovered she had pancreatic cancer. I'm not sure she wanted anyone to know. I didn't even find out that she had passed until after it happened—I read it in the online version of *The Los Angeles Times*!

I called her husband Roger to express my deep condolences. During our conversation, I asked him point blank why Lynn wouldn't tell me that she was ill. Roger had told me that in addition to the cancer, she had recently fallen in her bathtub and that injury contributed to her deteriorating health. I was on the verge of tears, and then when he told me, "Julia, Lynn didn't want to upset you because you were ... her daughter," I totally lost it and started bawling my head off.

Roger went on to say that Lynn had a number of keepsakes that were handed down to her from her mother and grandmother, various items of jewelry and other memorabilia that he knew Lynn would want me to have. Needless to say, not a day goes by when I don't think of her and I miss her terribly. She was a talented, beautiful actress and a kind, caring, loving person.

Many years after *Hazel* ended, I called Shirley. She was living in a cottage on Cape Cod, Massachusetts. As we spoke, she told me that she had gone completely blind and had tracks installed in her one-level house. Shirley had a chair attached to rollers, and the tracks would take her anywhere she needed to go in her home so she could care for herself without the need of assistance. She was still preparing her own meals and washing her own clothes, and she was completely self-sufficient. Shirley did have a housekeeper/maid that would come in once a month to clean the floors, vacuum, and do any heavy chores that needed to be done. Hazel Burke would be proud—what an amazing woman!

I asked her if she welcomed visitors, hoping she'd get the hint. She told me at this stage in her life, she was very happy just being by herself. I thanked her for everything she had done for me. She remarked that many people had told her I had grown into a beautiful young woman as well as a very good actress. I was sincerely humbled by the compliment.

Shirley passed away in 1992 at the age of 94. How very blessed I am to have had Shirley Booth as a part of my life at such a very young, impressionable age. I'm not sure she ever really knew how much she helped shape my career.

FADE OUT

CHAPTER 4 – ACTING MORE IN THE 1960S AND 1970S

After *Hazel*, I would go on to do many other TV roles. I was asked by producer Don Fedderson to work on *My Three Sons* in guest roles, one time as a student with a chemistry project with lots of lines, and another time to play Ernie's girlfriend, Margaret. There were no interviews for the part, just a direct hire.

I remember on that set that Barry Livingston, who played Ernie, used to sit in his dressing room and play his cello. We never really talked though except for the scenes we shot together. His brother, Stan Livingston, who played Chip, was nice and friendly, and Tina Cole, who played Robbie's wife Katie, was beautiful and sweet Tina. I saw Fred MacMurray only once on their set, overhearing him say as he was with the makeup and wardrobe people that he wanted to shoot the scene and get done quickly so he could carry on with his day.

I also was a guest star on a religious show called *This Is the Life*, also a Don Fedderson production that Don asked me to do with myself and a beautiful little black girl. The show was about how these little girls were friends but their parents wouldn't let them play together because of their different races.

Don came over to me himself and told me that my performance was more than he could have ever asked for. Of course it was a little confusing to me about the different colors of our skin regarding the episode, because the guards at the stage doors on Screen Gems were black, and they were Bobby's and my buddies. The show was critically acclaimed, and I remember how my mom and the little girl's mom talked and how my mom made her feel so at home and comfortable so we could play together and have a nice lunch. My mom was great, never teaching me any kind of hate and telling me that the word hate was an awful word and never to use it.

I had the pleasure to meet and work with Shirley Temple Black for a pilot she was doing appropriately called *The Shirley Temple Pilot*. Shirley was such a nice gal, and I remember I asked my mom if I could go and say hi to her. My mom said yes, so I walked over to her before the shoot and introduced myself to her and told her how much I loved all her shows when she was a little girl. Shirley and I shook hands, and she told me how much she loved my work too. She was so nice and so pretty.

During the shoot for the scene, which was about three little children banging on the bathroom door, crying and pleading for our mother to open the door and come out, the real mother of the youngest child kept walking onto the set and pushing me out of the scene in favor of her daughter. My mom walked over to that woman and told her that if she touched me or walked onto the scene one more time, my mom would have the director have the child taken out of the scene for good. The mother acted so badly that my mom had to tell her that I was the child star and not her daughter. The director, who was a friend of my dad, thanked my mom, and we finally shot the scene.

On the same show, my mother was played by Joyce Van Patten, a wonderful actress and nice woman who would bring me a bakery cookie after lunch that day. I just loved her, and she was a really good friend of my dad as well.

I also worked with Walter Brennan and Dack Rambo on *The Guns of Will Sonnett*. There was a scene where I was hiding behind a chair watching the fight scene, and my mom, my little brother and I had to leave the house and ride in a covered wagon with two horses. The carriage was creaky and the wooden wheels made so much noise and Ann Doran, who played my mom, drove the wagon with the horses so fast, it seemed like we were riding on one side of the wagon wheels when we made our turn out of the shot. Ann was another one of the nicest women to work with.

There was a scene with Dack too where he is grabbing us kids and pulling and dragging us back to the house, and we were fighting him all the way. He was so handsome and such a nice man, and I had such a big crush on him during our shoot.

Walter was so funny. When I went to introduce myself to him, in his cranky fashion, he looked at me and asked me if I knew my lines. I said yes, then he gave me that wink and told me to go and play as we were shooting on the back lot. It was so hot and dusty, but I had a great time, because I got to pet the horses and the handler let me sit on top of one of his horses and take a ride.

The horses were truly gentle giants, and I would then go on to take riding lessons from Johnny Carpenter, a stuntman who catered horses to the studio. Johnny was just wonderful, and the horse he trained me on was called Black Jack. I learned how to ride western and bareback, and the minute Johnny put me up on his horse, he told my mother that I had a natural seat on a horse and he couldn't believe that was my first time on a horse.

I really loved Johnny, he was so rugged and handsome. He was a very gentle, quiet and patient man at his Pioneer Town in California, where he taught disabled children how to ride. Johnny was a treasure of a man. He would take me on long rides through his ranch and told me when we started that a horseman didn't talk on the trail—that we had to keep our eyes open and watch for snakes and critters that were on the trail. When I asked him if we could gallop, he told me, "Julia, OK, but I don't want my horses coming back ridden hard and put up wet." When I told him I didn't know what that meant, he said he'd show me, and when we got back, he taught me how to take the saddles off, clean the hoofs, never to stand behind the horses, and mount on the left side.

We brushed and cooled the horses down before they were taken back into the stables because it was hot there. He also taught me how to barrel race and slide off the back of a horse, and I was good at it too. After each lesson, he always told me to say hi to my dad and what a wonderful father I had, and how many people loved him and depended on him for jobs and their health insurance with the Screen Actors Guild. He always gave me a kiss and hug when I left and said, "Come see Uncle Johnny soon." I just couldn't wait to come back.

My next job was working on *Mr. and Mrs. Bo Jo Jones*, a movie of the week on the 20th Century lot. Dan Dailey played the father, Dina Merrill the mother, Christopher Norris my big sister and I was Grace, the young daughter. Desi Arnaz Jr. played Christopher's boyfriend. Eddie Foy III was our casting director, and he asked me to come in and say hi to him before he cast me for the part and gave me my script. They wanted to strip my hair and dye my hair blonde to be a better match for the cast, but the studio decided against it. My ABC advisor for this was Allen Epstein, a very well-known and famous producer in Hollywood and a really big man. Everyone called him "The Bear."

Our first scene was shot in a beautiful house, with Dina, Christopher and myself in the kitchen, I got to wear my roller skates for the scene and had lots of fun skating back and forth during the scene. I remember how wonderful and beautiful Chris was and so very friendly and sweet.

I can't say the same about Dina, although she was a very beautiful and elegant woman, not a hair out of place and beautiful wardrobe. When I asked my mom if it was OK to introduce myself and say hi, she warned me that Dina was a very rich woman and probably wouldn't receive me well. I visited Dina when she was in makeup at the Malibu church location shoot at the top of the hill that overlooked Pepperdine University and was used frequently in Hollywood. She had no interest in talking with a child at all and asked me to go away. When I talked to my mom about this, she assured me that not all people are nice or happy or even like children, even professional children, and added, "Julia, you have one thing that no one can take away from you, good manners, and that they will take you anywhere you want to go in life, anywhere, you can sit at a table with king and queens, presidents, or the richest people in the world and feel right at home."

So that was that, and I found something else to do and never spoke to Dina off the set again, and even that seemed to bother her. I didn't know she was one of the richest woman in the world at that time, and a true socialite, that most people bowed down to her.

My mother did go over to Dina, introduced herself as Phil Benjamin's wife and apologized and told her that I would never talk to her again during our shoot. Dina seemed to be bewildered at my mom's bold action, but my mom wasn't impressed with anybody, and she taught me never to be impressed or feel less than anyone no matter who they were. That would carry me all through my life.

My mom, no matter where we shot, always brought her book and knitting and crochet with her and always sat in the back and watched, dressed with her stockings and heels, pearls and earrings. Like a lady, her shoes were dyed to match all her dresses. She said few words to anyone unless they came up to talk with her, and then it was always like everyone was an old friend, and most people were.

During the shoot, we had a dinner scene table with Dan, Dina, Christopher, Desi and myself that was very tense, as Dan couldn't hear very well at all, and it took some time to shoot the scene. Dina seemed unhappy and so was the director. I did try to introduce myself to Desi, who was very quiet and shy but so very handsome, but this was not a happy set.

We finally shot it, and that was a wrap for me and my part on the show. As always, my mom insisted that I thank the director and the producer for having me on the show before I left and shake hands with the cast and crew. *Hazel* was so very different in atmosphere, and I was happy to go home and go swimming in our heated pool in our backyard and play afterward.

I also was on *The Paul Lynde Show* and *The New Andy Griffith Show* for a day's work, very small scenes on both. I was wearing braces at this point, so there really wasn't too much work available at that time for me. I remember how very funny Paul was on the set and off, just a happy man in a big playground, and how nice and kind Andy was on his show as well.

Hollywood really is a gift. I feel very sad for all the child stars and actors that didn't enjoy their time in Hollywood, because it has given many of them the platform to carry on for most if not all for the rest of the years in their lives. Yes, Hollywood is work, but folks, let me tell you, so are many other professions in life. The securities industry is as tough as it gets. I have no regrets working in that industry either, as it gave me great life lessons on how to manage money and understand how money really never does rest. It's in a constant flow, all around the world, buy or a sell.

CHAPTER 5 – HAPPY IN HAWAII, UNHAPPY AT HOME

My dad was under contract at 20th Century Fox by the late 1960s, casting *Tora, Tora, Tora*. The studio sent all of us to Hawaii where they were casting and shooting the movie. My dad left before us and went to set us up at the Halekulani Hotel in Oahu on Waikiki Beach. At that time, the Halekulani had bungalows all around the property for suites to live in. It was beautiful. Our whole family went, as my dad came back to get my mom, sister, grandmother and me and we flew to Hawaii together.

As my dad casting a lot of the movie from our bungalow, I would read with the actors for him. Then he would help me with my schoolwork. It was truly heaven, and first class all the way, I learned to surf and snorkel. The studio gave my mom a very generous expense account/per diem to go shopping and pay for our entertainment, and I had a credit on file to eat at the little café on the beach. It was wonderful.

Every day, we went to the hotel restaurant for breakfast outside on the patio, it was so beautiful. The executive chef would always come out to say good morning to all of us, especially my dad, because everyone on the island wanted to be a part of the movie, and my dad saw everyone. The food was delicious, and the fruit was out of this world. My dad loved his fresh fruit and good hot coffee with my mom, and the waiters made sure they had plenty and enough to take back to our hut for the day. My mom loved to smoke her cigarettes on the patio and look out at the beautiful water while we casually dined. Then it was time for my dad and me to start the casting session for the entire day until early midafternoon, when we'd break and then I'd work on my homework.

Unfortunately, it wasn't very long that we had arrived when my grandma and my sister had to head back to the mainland. My grandma really wasn't in good health, and she missed her bulldog and my poodle Susie and really just the house in general. My sister just wanted to go home. She didn't enjoy our luxurious trip at all, and she has always been a homebody, no desire to leave California at all, just wanted to be with her boyfriends. There was just no way to keep my sister and grandmother happy no matter how much money, shopping and gifts they got while treating them to a very nice lifestyle. They left as my mom and I stayed with my dad for the next nine months and had the time of our lives. In fact my parents were talking about retiring to Hawaii and even started to make some plans.

One evening after my grandma and sister had left, my dad, mom and I went to go see Don Ho and his band the Allis at Duke Kahanamoku's International Marketplace for dinner. Don asked me to come up on stage and sing with him and another girl, and it didn't take Don very long to instantly recognize I had a singing voice. He asked if I would do a song for the troops that were in house that evening, so I sang "Where Have All the Flowers Gone" with Don and the Allis backing me up. The troops just loved my singing, and everyone in the audience started to cry by the end of my song and gave me a standing ovation. We had a wonderful evening, and after Don's set, he and my dad sat in Don's booth and discussed their business about the movie. My mom and I went shopping in the marketplace until my dad was finished, then we took our taxi back to the Halekulani Hotel.

When we returned home, I had a very difficult time, as I went back to public school after leaving Hollywood Professional School and Hawaii. It really was unpleasant. The kids were such horrible bullies, and so were the teachers. I was asked constantly by grown-ups how much money I made, why would a rich girl be in a regular school, why wasn't I working, why my dad or mom didn't drive expensive cars, and so on. It was always something and I never really fit in, and so during this time it was very lonely and nothing that I was used to, having no friends really.

Also, we had a lot of problems at home with my sister Betty. Being there was filled with tension and unhappy times. Betty seemed to be always in trouble and rebelling. To be home with my grandma was also hard, because grandma was always drinking and popping pills, so you never knew what mood she was in, plus my mom was very addicted to pain pills and you never knew what mood she was in either. My grandma and mom were always grounding my sister and hitting her in punishment, and it was a terrible thing to watch.

My sister's rebellious streak began years earlier. I remember that when I was about four or five, my sister and a girl in the neighborhood down the street took me and we ran away. My dad was out in his car looking for us and so was everyone else. We were in matching black pants and black-and-white diamond checker tops walking miles away from our house. Every time that we saw the police car coming, we would hide between the houses. Finally, we were so far away from home and I was so tired that I had to go to the bathroom, so we saw a gas station on the corner of a dirt road. Across the street was a fruit and vegetable outside stand where we used to go and get our corn in the summer. As we crossed the street and went inside, my dad happened to see us in our outfits and pulled into the gas station, opened the bathroom door and got us into the car and drove us back home.

I was really tired and was happy to come home, but when we got back, my grandma gave my sister the worst beating, with her over her knee and her panties down, until I screamed at her to stop. I was crying so much because I didn't know if she was going to spank me next (she didn't), but it was awful, and as my sister grew up, it wasn't long before she started running away from home all the time.

Now, I was about eleven or twelve and not working as much while my sister was four years older and hated being home. She was always in trouble for wearing miniskirts, black makeup and teased hair. Betty was known as a low rider and a very tough girl, so no one really bothered her, and she had no problem letting people know that.

One time when she ran away, it was early evening and we were in our bedroom which was at the back of the house close to the garage. My grandma had piled wood up on a table so you couldn't open the back gate near us, which also was locked. I saw three people over the fence, and they kept calling my sister's name, slowly and softly as a whisper, almost like a chant, saying, "Betty, Betty, come with us." They kept repeating this until my sister told me to be very quiet while she packed up a small bag of her things, pried opened the screen and crawled out the bedroom window. She told me not to say a thing for fifteen minutes until she was long gone or she'd beat me up, and made her bed look like someone was sleeping in it. I didn't say a word.

The people on the other side of the fence were two girls and one guy with long black hair. They were so creepy, and I was really scared, but mostly because I didn't know how my mom and grandma and dad would react. It wasn't long before my mom came into our room and saw that the screen was bent open and Betty was gone again, this time longer than all the other occasions.

My dad was still working at 20th Century Fox at the time, and he had the studio security, the FBI and federal authorities look for her. He and I would get in his car and go around the neighborhood to find her or visit her friends' houses and asking if they knew where she was. It was so sad, because my dad cried so much and he loved Betty when we were growing up so much more than me.

People spotted Betty at Pandora's Box and other Hollywood hot spots, but she always seemed to leave just before the police or feds would get there—until she was picked up five hours before they found Charles Manson at his Spawn Ranch right after the La-Bianca murders. Betty was found inside a closet inside the Spawn Ranch house and had peed her pants, and officers said she had been in the closet for at least five hours and was so scared.

The search for Betty just about turned 20th Century Fox upside down and almost to a halt while they were looking for her. Eddie Foy III, who was my casting director for *Mr. and Mrs. Bo Jo Jones*, talked about this with me many years later when I saw him for the first time after his wife died and we were at the Donna Reed Festival for young performers, where I was teaching a voice class. He told me that the studio had almost completely shut down while they were looking for Betty, as my dad had hired all studio people to hunt her down and find her, at any cost. All my money that I made from acting was used to pay for this, and after she did come back home, pregnant at fifteen or sixteen, more of my money was used to fly her to Mexico City for a botched abortion that made her so very sick when she came back home.

It was awful, and it was then she met her dirty husband, a real creep who wanted to marry her but wouldn't leave me alone. He was always sitting outside in his lowered green Chevy at my junior and senior high schools, waiting for me to come out, telling me my parents had sent him to pick me up from school and then taking me up to the Chatsworth mountains to get me drunk on strawberry wine and molest me. He was disgusting, he stunk from decayed teeth and just poor hygiene. To avoid him, I told my mom and dad that I wouldn't go back to school—and didn't. I dropped out the first ten weeks of eleventh grade and finished at a vocational school, and by that time Betty was long gone from our house, living with him and his poor family from Mexico in a rundown house in San Fernando.

Betty said she was happy amongst her new family roots. Believe me, as a beautiful, five-foot-seven blonde rich girl, Betty had every opportunity to have everything I did and more. Many young men in Hollywood would have been proud to have her as a wife and wanted to date her, but she always liked the dirtiest guys, so her choice was her own.

Soon they eloped, and Betty didn't care how she got what she wanted. She forged my dad's name to buy her house and took everything—and I mean everything—of my earnings. Years later Betty took the proceeds from my mom's house after my dad died, her car, and kept her in the backyard of a dirty two-bedroom add-on in the Palmdale house that she and her husband built when they moved from San Fernando so as upon selling they would benefit from the proceeds, leaving my mom nothing.

During that time when Betty got married, I went to stay with Eddie Foy and his wife, but soon they went through a terrible divorce and she died. I wasn't staying with them when she died; I had gone back home, and soon my grandma moved out to an assisted living home very close to our house. My Aunt Izzy from my mother's side came down from San Jose and moved my grandmother in with her and her husband Ray, a black man who was the nicest man ever. Izzy had five children, but this interracial marriage really was a big secret in our family that upset my grandmother so much in the early years. Nonetheless, she moved in with them.

My mom was quite upset with the recent upheavals at home, including my dad being out of work for a short time. He and I tried to put the pieces for the three of us back together. I got a job down the street at a local supermarket bagging groceries by telling them I was older than I was. That helped out a lot. I would take my entire paycheck, cash it out at the store, and bring home food and cigarettes for my mom. Soon my dad was back casting again, and I took classes at the vocational center for front office, back office and medical transcribing and terminology. One class I just loved was called Face, Figure and Fashion.

After that, I soon was working at Children's Hospital in Los Angeles and received a scholarship for twenty-five thousand dollars to study radiology, but my dad wanted me to come back to work in Hollywood. I went back to doing voiceovers and many guest roles on TV and commercials.

CHAPTER 6 – GETTING BACK INTO ACTING

I landed a guest starring role on *House Calls*, which my dad was casting at Universal Studios. I had so much fun working on that series with Wayne Rogers and Lynn Redgrave. Lynn was so funny. When she came up to introduce herself to me, she said, "Hi, I'm Lynn Redgrave, please don't hold my sister Vanessa against me!" (I loved Vanessa in the movie *Julia*, so it was no problem.)

It was a really fun shoot about a couple who got married on roller skates and the wife (me) broke her leg. My husband kept trying to sneak into the hospital room for our first night together. It was a hilarious episode to, and everyone had a great time on that set when we performed it too.

At the same time I worked on *House Calls*, I had a commercial running called "Take Five Little Casseroles." It was a couple on roller skates doing a spot for a cup of soup, and I had all the dialogue. It was fun. We went to Frederick's of Hollywood for our wardrobe, and I used my own skates that were custom fit for me from Northridge Skate Rink when I was skating in competitions, plus I had used them in a national commercial we shot in San Francisco on roller skates in the park. We shot all day and flew home that night. We were sure tired on the plane trip, but all of us that shot it laughed and had a great time on the flight regardless.

Speaking of roller skating, one of the things I loved to do was roller skate when I was about fifteen. A group of us would meet every Friday and Saturday night for the evening sessions. It was our social circle and just plain good clean fun. I would also start to take lessons and compete as a skater in competitions around California—we all did. The owner and his wife were just wonderful, and I dated their younger son for a short time. All the girls had a crush on his older brother, and we all got a chance to work for them too in the snack bar or as skate guards for the guys. After we were done, we'd all go to an ice cream parlor or a restaurant. I met a girlfriend there, and we would go to Zuma Beach all the time and then to the rink, but soon she would get married and we wouldn't talk for many years later. Facebook is great, because I had the chance to meet and catch up with all my childhood friends from skating.

I would continue to work back in the industry also appearing in more episodic TV and voice work. I worked on *Testimony of Two Men*, a TV miniseries that was a period drama in which I was dressed for my part in a post-Civil War costume dress, which is always fun in Hollywood. Another TV miniseries called *Loose Change* had me portray a rocker girl with a fun costume and glitter makeup, then I was dressed very conservatively for a guest shot on *Kingston Confidential* with Raymond Burr. I remember that Raymond was such a nice man and good friends of my father.

The best part of growing up in Hollywood is you never know what part you will land, so it's always exciting to see what your wardrobe, makeup and hair will be, because it's not up to you to decide. Just show up on time, hit your mark and know your lines. I always did.

CHAPTER 7 – CLOSE ENCOUNTERS OF THE FAMOUS KIND

I was so very privileged to work for Stephen J. Cannell and his writers including David Chase on *The Rockford Files* for two episodes. "Black Mirror" was a two-part drama from Stephen, David, J. Rickley Dumm, Chas. Floyd Johnson and Meta Rosenberg where I played the role of Bonnie, a very troubled young girl seeing her psychiatrist. For "The Prisoner of Rosemont Hall," written by Stephen, David, Chas. Floyd and Meta, Jim Garner actually requested me to play the part of a young student named Melinda, as it involved a rape scene, and he didn't want to have to worry about working with someone he didn't know or trust.

While Jim and I were getting ready to shoot our scene on "The Prisoner of Rosemont Hall," which was on location at a college, we were in the classroom behind the closed doors preparing for the scene, and as we were standing listening for our queue, I can't tell how tall and handsome and manly Jim was. I had a breakaway on my T-shirt for the scene that I would tear down and scream rape, then head out the classroom door. He was checking to make sure that my blouse was ready because, he told me, "Julia, honey, I only want to shoot this scene once." We did that, and after that he was looking at me and told me so sweetly, "Julia, you're a heartbreaker. Honey, you're just beautiful." I've worked with a lot of great actors, but none have ever compared to Jim Garner, such a nice man and a class act, so very down to earth.

When I would work on his show he would come to my dressing room, which was a trailer, after makeup and knock on my trailer door, even if the door was open. He'd say, "Hi Julia, honey, thank you for being on my show today." I really was shocked the first time he did that and couldn't wait to tell my dad, who had his casting office on the Universal lot too. Also, when I saw him in the makeup room, he would wait until the makeup man finished his work and then take tissues and rub it all off. When I saw him do this, I started to laugh and asked him what he was doing. He told me, "Now Julia, you know real men don't wear makeup, not me anyway," and he got such a kick out of me laughing that we both started laughing together. He gave me a big hug and asked me if I was ready to shoot, and I said yes I was. Jimmie was the kind of man to make any girl weak in the knees, and he will always be one of my favorite actors of all time.

It was such a thrill to be a part of *The Rockford Files*, a gifted show with such wonderful people who were happy and enjoying their work, and each and every person on the crew made each episode a success. I would have the privilege to work with Stephen J. Cannell on some of his other projects too—*The Jordan Chance*, again with Raymond Burr, *The Rousters*, another fun show to work on, and *Riptide*, where I played the role of Nurse Fiske, who sees Joe Penny for the first time and goes completely starry-eyed with a big crush on him in the scene. That was a fun shoot, because I really hammed it up and made the whole cast and crew laugh while we were shooting.

I worked on *General Hospital* several times, being hired by the late casting director Marvin Paige, who I had the opportunity to see after many years later at Cantor's Deli on Fairfax, where he invited me and a friend to watch the *2001: A Space Odyssey* in 70mm at the Academy of Motion Picture Arts and Sciences' Samuel Goldwyn Theater. Marvin and I both had a hot pastrami, and when I ordered my hot sandwich with Swiss, he looked at me and said, "Cheese on pastrami?!" And immediately I said, "No, not cheese, just pastrami on rye, please." He looked at me and said, "That's better, Julia. You still look beautiful." I asked him, "Are pickles OK?" and he said yes, and we had a great time. You had to love Marvin, one of the good ole boys in casting in Hollywood.

I would also work from time to time on *The Young and the Restless* for a few recurring times as a day player, as a nurse again. The day after I saw Marvin, we went to the book signing of Jeanne Cooper, who played Katherine Chancellor on *The Young and the Restless*, a great friend of my dad and mom's for many years as well as working for my dad. When I went up to say hi to her, I knew she was very sick, but she took my hands in hers with tears in her eyes, and nothing needed to be said when I told her I was Phil Benjamin's daughter. Jeanne was truly one of the Hollywood great actresses we had, everyone loved her and she is dearly missed.

I would go on to work constantly in voiceovers, dubbing and dialects, of which I had mastered and truly enjoyed doing. Many times as I drove on the lots of Universal, Warner Bros., Quinn Martin, MGM, 20th Century Fox, I would sign several time cards at once, doing various voices for many different TV shows or movies.

As a child, my mom would drive me when I did the voice of the "Little Bo Peep" doll, where you would pull the cord on the back of her head to make her talk. She was a pretty little old fashioned doll. Security was really tight there. You really were frisked by the guard as you walked into the building to go to the sound room, even for a small child and performer to come into the building. Cameras were everywhere, as were toys, but you were not allowed to touch anything.

My mom also drove me on several occasions to the Disney lot, and of course that is just a dream come true for a child to see, just like walking into Disneyland, so clean and colorful, with all the classic Disney characters pointing at the numbers for each soundstage. One time I was there and saw Kurt Russell, so handsome and always happy and waving hi to me. I had the best time walking through the soundstage with Walt, who was happy and waving hello too. I worked with Disney's casting director, Virginia Martindale, a great gal.

My voiceover dubbing credits for 1970s and 1980s TV series are many—*The Incredible Hulk, Simon & Simon, Magnum P.I., BJ and the Bear, Emergency, The Dukes of Hazzard, Sheriff Lobo, Buck Rogers in the 25th Century, Young Maverick, Enos, Tenspeed and Brownshoe, Otherworld, The Gangster Chronicles, Cassie & Co., Private Benjamin, Whiz Kids, Tales of the Gold Monkey, The Four Seasons* and *Murder She Wrote*. I also did voiceovers for the TV movies and miniseries *V, The Last Convertible*, and the movies *Dead and Buried* and *Cheech and Chong's "Nice Dreams"* and *"Up In Smoke,"* all done in Hollywood. There was also a Shakespeare production at the Old Globe Theatre, *Much Ado About Nothing*, where I played Hero. I would also shoot many commercials in Hollywood too.

CHAPTER 8 – HOW MOM AND DAD MET

My dad was so instrumental and thrilled I was back at work. He was a great man in Hollywood and loved by so many people in the industry. He had an interesting background. His family migrated from Australia to San Francisco, where he was born. His father's name was Percy Mayer Benjamin, and his mother's name was Grace Ladd Ostrander. Percy was a butcher/salesman, and Grace was a housewife.

I remember my father telling me how young he was when he started working. First he sold newspapers on the corner of Fairfax and Beverly in Hollywood. I remember this because he told me he had to fight with his fists to keep his corner every day against bullies he called "stumblebums." Then he worked in a potato chip factory to put himself through high school.

His mother died when he was only thirteen years old from cancer, either breast or ovarian. He and his dad struggled very hard to live, and they used to buy damaged fruits and vegetables to eat because they were cheap. After his mother died, he also stayed with an aunt and after he had his meals he would leave a nickel under his plate.

Dad went on to finish school at Fairfax High and then put himself through college at the University of Southern California, where he played football and received his business administration degree. He graduated in 1934. Universal Pictures employed my dad as an assistant casting director for ten years until February 26, 1943, the date when he entered the Army as a public relations writer.

It was in the Army where my dad and mom met, put on productions for our troops and eventually married. My mom told me that while she was working in the Army for a corporal doing office duty, my dad used to come by her office and just stare at her in his oversized uniform every day and ask her to go out with him. She told me she always said no, but her Army friends and WACS would tell her she was crazy and why not just go out for one date. Of course that one date turned into marriage.

My mom enlisted in the Army underage. She was a nightclub singer in Madison, Wisconsin, when she married a man who she said was a terrible alcoholic and his mother was very mean to her. To get away from those bad memories, my grandmother drove her to the station to enlist in service for World War II.

Both my parents, Ronald Reagan and Tony Curtis all met in the Army at that time and began putting shows on in Camp Haan in Riverside, California, a show called *Grins and Bitters*, where my both my parents received letters of appreciation dated June 30, 1945, in recognition of selling war bonds at that show. My dad's letter reads:

Cpl. Phil Benjamin
c/o Major Daniel F. Deedy
Special Services Offices
Camp Haan
Riverside California

Dear Cpl. Benjamin:

In appreciation of your splendid assistance in connection with the sale of war bonds, may I present to you the enclosed United States Treasury citation on behalf of the War Finance Committee for Southern California. We are extremely appreciative of the fine cooperation you rendered the Treasury Department during the 7th War Loan by assisting so graciously as a member of the cast in the stage production *Grins and Bitters*. You are to be congratulated most enthusiastically on your patriotic attitude, and it is through the splendid cooperation of people like you that Southern California is able to maintain its outstanding record for bond sales.

Sincerely,

George Harshberger, Jr.
Promotional Director

My mother would also receive her letter of appreciation:

Miss Tony Beaumont
C/o Major Daniel F. Deedy
Special Services Offices
Camp Haan
Riverside, California

Dear Miss Beaumont:

In appreciation of your splendid assistance in connection with the sale of war bonds, may I present to you the enclosed United States Treasury citation on behalf of the War finance Committee for Southern California. We are extremely appreciative of the fine cooperation you rendered the Treasury Department during the 7th War Loan by assisting so graciously as a "Bomb-n-Dear" in the stage production *Grins and Bitters*. You are to be congratulated most enthusiastically on your patriot attitude, and it is through the splendid cooperation of people like you that Southern California is able to maintain its outstanding record for bond sales.

Sincerely,
George Harshberger, Jr.

My parents married October 14, 1945 at Chapel-Chapman Park Hotel in Los Angeles. My father received his honorable discharge February 18, 1946, and resumed his casting career at Universal Studios for over five decades. This would be the last place he would work before his death.

My mom and dad had so much fun together at the studios. They loved to go and watch Ronald Reagan shoot the Bonzo movies he was casting; have drinks and dinner with (Bud) Abbott and (Lou) Costello, Gracie Allen and George Burns, and Steve Allen and Jayne Meadows; and go marlin fishing with Dick and Darryl Zanuck on their private yacht.

The studio was so much fun. One time all the executives dressed up as the female stars on the lot for an evening gala, and you could tell who my dad was because he left on his argyle socks in his Hawaiian costume.

At one point my dad was a great friend of William Powell, president of Four Star Studios, and they were going to open up a studio together. Unfortunately, William became very ill of cancer during their plans and died, which really devastated my dad.

As casting director, Dad worked with director Billy Wilder on picking the actors the latter's movies *Some Like it Hot*, *The Apartment* and *Irma La Douce* (Dad adored Shirley MacLaine). He also worked with director Robert Wise years to help cast *The Sound of Music*. There are so many more casting jobs to his credit, with hundreds of TV shows plus the movies *Paint Your Wagon*, *The Flim Flan Man*, *The Dirty Dozen*, *The Sand Pebbles*, *Stagecoach* (the 1966 remake), *Hello, Dolly!*, *Star!*, *Tora! Tora! Tora!*, *Doctor Doolittle*, *Willy Wonka and the Chocolate Factory* and *Ode to Billie Joe*.

I remember my dad told me that he and Ronald Reagan helped write some of the Screen Actors Guild rules. My mother told me that the Mafia tried to take our union, and my dad and Ronnie walked right in and told them they would have to shoot them in the back on their way out before they would let them take our union. They walked out.

When Menahem Golan and Yoram Globus came to Hollywood with $100 million to make movies, my father cast their first films (*Lepke* and *The Four Deuces*) and showed them the ropes on how to get started. Of course, when I called them after they were a huge success, they had no idea who Phil Benjamin was.

Dad told me of the time he fought hard for Frank Sinatra to be cast at the studio, and when Frank was finally hired, he handed my father a blank check and told him to fill in whatever amount he wanted. My dad brought the check home to show my mom, but they decided to hand it back to Frank with their most humble thanks the next day. That's the kind of people my dad and mom were.

My mom loved to take me to the yearly Motion Picture Television mothers' luncheon at the Beverly Hills Hotel, where we always sat with Edith Head, the Academy Award-winning costume designer. The proceeds went to the Motion Picture Television Hospital in Woodland Hills and the Motion Picture Relief Fund. Since I was twenty-one, I have donated a part of my entire residuals to the Motion Picture Television Hospital. Although there really wasn't any of my money left from working as a child star, my mom always made sure we had beautiful lunches at the best department stores where we would shop, or stop at a coffee shop for a piece of warm pie and coffee after an interview until the traffic would let up to drive back home to the San Fernando Valley.

My grandmother, who lived with us by my dad's request for my mom, really was a piece of work. She came to live with us when I was about two from a small house she bought in San Fernando—I remember there was an outhouse in the back yard. She loved and raised her bulldogs; there was Duff, Sam, Hangover, Shotsy, Penelope Sugar and Cinderella.

Grandma loved the horse races and bet regularly on Saturday nights. She had a really nice cream-colored wooden station wagon with a bulldog emblem on the hood, and she would take my sister and me down to Van Nuys in the evenings to pick up her racing forms so she could bet. A lot of my dad's friends from the studio joined in too. After Grandma got her racing forms, we'd stop and get an ice cream cone for the ride back, and what a ride it was.

Her name was Isabel Farwell, but everyone called her Hortense. Boy, did she ever drink and take a bunch of pills all the time. Grandma did a lot of the cooking at our house, and when she was good, it was great, and when she was bad, it was awful. But she really was funny, and my, what a character.

My grandmother, and my grandfather that I never met, worked in vaudeville. She played a lot of instruments—piano, accordion, and clarinet—and would put on the craziest costumes and come out from her room to the den and do song and dance numbers for our family in the loudest colors and skimpiest lingerie outfits known to man. She would put on her cherry earrings and red lipstick all over her mouth and do her routine for my dad on weekends.

Sometimes Grandma would even take me to an interview, and she would drive all over the road, high as can be. Then there were times when you would go into her room in our house and it looked like a Roman torch in there—candles lit, incense burning—and she was always making something, so there was glue and glitter everywhere. Come Christmastime, our house was decorated everywhere, especially the den, as her handmade glittery ornaments were huge and were hanging all over the ceiling.

Grandma loved witchcraft and her tarot cards. She gave astrological and numerology readings to many people in her lifetime. Also, every once in a while the Devonshire police would come knocking on our door, my dad would answer and invite the policemen in for a beer while Grandma got dressed and got her purse to take a little ride to the station to be booked for gambling. She and my dad spent a lot of time in her room, placing bets and using her tarot cards for advice.

So there you have it, folks. My sister is climbing out the bedroom window, Grandma's betting and getting pinched from time to time, and Mom became very addicted to pain pills for her hip and acute migraines, while Dad and I are working at the studio. My house kept getting nuttier than a fruitcake. Home baked.

CHAPTER 9 – FINDING ROMANCE AND DISAPPOINTMENT

When I was nineteen and in early twenties, I got my first apartment in Oxnard, a duplex right on the beach where I had a beautiful unobstructed view of the Channel Islands. I would go there when I was finished shooting or done with interviews for the week with my dog, Cyrano De Bergerac, who I got from Actors and Others for Animals. The lady next door to my parents lost her Basset Hound, and when Cyrano just wasn't the perfect replacement for her, I took him in along with my big red kitty, Redman, who came from a litter that my sister had with her husband's family in San Fernando under the house.

I really loved my animals so much, and when I needed to come back to Los Angeles for work, we'd all three get in the car and I would stay at my mom and dad's house in Calabasas. They sold their house in Granada Hills and bought a very large mobile home. A couple of years later, my dad would be diagnosed with kidney cancer. He had his kidney removed and lived another three and one half years after that.

Down the street from their mobile home was a gas station. A young man who worked there as a mechanic would always come out, say hi and fill my gas tank for me and look under the hood. He was always asking my dad for my address to come and see me, as he loved to surf. Tall and handsome, he was a really nice guy but very weak, and I would later find out he took a lot of drugs too. Many times my dad refused to give my number to him until one day I asked him to change his mind, and we talked after that.

The duplex where I was living in at the beach soon gave me a quit notice after that, because the owners wanted it back for themselves, and I sure couldn't blame them. A child star who was younger than me lived with his grandma there, and he would visit me all the time. We would be friends forever. I went to his wedding, and when his beautiful wife became pregnant, my mom suggested the name for his first child, a son.

So I moved back to Los Angeles to Beachwood Canyon in Hollywood. I started dating the handsome man from the gas station, who asked if he could move in with me. Soon after, I was pregnant with my son, Branden, and we were going to get married, but he walked out two weeks before our wedding. He left me a note on my car that read;

Dear Julia,

I am very sorry for the way things turned out, but I think it is for the best. I love you, but I think everything went a little too fast, and I'm scared. I just finished with a long-term ill-fated relationship which ended in disaster, and I am afraid it will happen again. You are a good person and will make someone a good wife. I am just not ready now. I hope you understand.

I cannot express my feelings in words about how I feel now, but all I ask is for your forgiveness. I'm sorry my car is still in the parking place. The battery is dead. I will come down to get it either tonight or tomorrow. I'll call before I come.

Love,
Rick
Take care of yourself.

Now, at the time I was studying comedy with the number one coach for comedy in Hollywood. It wasn't easy to get into his class either. First you had to audit his class for six months before you even got to be considered for one of his classes, and so I did. I would study with him for over three years. You had to be good, very good to be a part of his workshop. All the best actors were studying with him, including Robin Williams.

Unfortunately, one night towards the end of my pregnancy, my son's father showed up at the class high and drunk, talking with my coach and the other actors there. I was so embarrassed, I really wanted to hide somewhere, and that would be the last time I attended the best training comedy class there was in Hollywood. Not too long after that, our brilliant coach died. I did continue to work in voiceovers until about two weeks prior to giving birth to my son.

I really had a hard pregnancy, with morning sickness all nine months long. His family was just awful, really narrow minded, negative and very cynical plus very controlling of their son. We lived together while I was pregnant in a house my dad was going to buy us in Woodland Hills. The house belonged to an agent friend of my dad's whose brother had passed away. It was really nice, a three-bedroom house with a nice pool and close to the 101 freeway, which was good for me to get to work.

But his family just wouldn't let us live our lives together, leaving constant messages and notes on our cars. His father even called my mother and said that they thought it was good idea if they handled all my money. That didn't go over well with my mom. In fact, she warned them that they better leave me alone immediately. So I decided to have my baby, not marry by his choice, and become a single parent.

Indeed, there wasn't one day of my pregnancy that his family didn't harass me, insisting that their son wasn't the father of my unborn child and that answering machines are for whores. They were always asking me about how much money I had just made, because I continued to work all the way up until the ninth month of my pregnancy until I gave birth.

Right after I gave birth to my son, just two weeks, I came home from my parents' house and found my son's father and his sister doing cocaine at my living room table. I put my baby in his crib—which by the way is the only thing his father ever bought him, and not one penny of child support either—walked over to the table, wiped the cocaine off it with my hand and threw them both out.

My son's father never came back. I moved in for a short time with my parents until I took a small single apartment in Studio City to be close to the studio and not too far from my dad, who was dying of cancer.

As it turned out, my son was the spitting image of his father, and his family said that they wanted me to forgive and forget the hell they put me through and all the horrible things they had said over the last nine months. I refused them. My father was so very sick by that time, and he died six months after I gave birth to my son, so I decided to go it alone. I just didn't need the problems, and I think it's not fair for a child to endure a lot of negativity and fighting; it's just not healthy.

I wished my son's father would have been strong and grown up to be a part of his life, but he wasn't. On a couple of occasions my son and I would run into him skiing or hanging at the beach, but he ran away from us. We tried to leave him a message and a phone number, but he was too scared and wanted nothing to do with his son. I was very unhappy and sad for my son even to this day, because we are good people and not anybody you would be ashamed to be seen with. My boy is truly a Benjamin, and I know how much this hurts him.

So his father not only broke my heart, but my son's heart too—twice. It's his loss.

Richard George Wheeler died 2/24/2015.

Regardless, I love being a parent, it's the best thing I have ever done, even though at that time it cost me a lot in my career. I would do it again—it made me whole as a woman.

CHAPTER 10 – LOSING DAD

During the time I moved back to Los Angeles from the beach, there was an actress who was all over my dad and many of the other producers, directors and high-profile actors in Hollywood. She was just plain bad news, always screwing anybody she could and always with married men, never a guy of her own. She appears throughout my life, and every time she appears, something always awful happens. I don't ever remember anyone in Hollywood so hateful, jealous and destructive as her, and there are some haters out there.

My father had hired her on a few occasions as an actress, and she was awful. One very well-known actor and comedian, a three-time Emmy winner who has since passed away, had her in his show, and he and his friend invited me and her to fly to Vegas for a weekend. This actor had gotten us a beautiful two-bedroom suite with a private pool, and when the guys went to gamble, she lost complete control of herself. The actor/comedian really liked me, and when they left to gamble that morning, she jumped on my back by the pool and started hitting me and pulling my hair, so I got right on a plane and came back home that day. When the actor called and I said why I left I told him, he told me he had asked the actress many times to get some help. At the end of the conversation, he asked me did I use the hundred dollars he left for me to go shopping while they were gambling. I told him I didn't know anything about that, and he expressed how disgusted and disappointed he was with her and again how badly she needed help.

A frequent co-worker with me in voiceovers for years told me to beware this gal. How right she was, as you will see.

This was a really sad time for me, as my dad was asked to leave Universal by a man who my dad trained who took over as head of casting. He dismissed my father with all his years and experience in Hollywood, and he wasn't very nice to the others that were working there. He even tried to fire the gal who was the receptionist, but my dad fought hard for her so she could keep her job and benefits.

One day before my dad was asked to leave the studio, we were having lunch together in the commissary when my acting coach yelled to him across the crowded room and said, "Hey Phil, your daughter is getting goddamn good!" That pleased my dad so much, I can't remember him ever smiling so long. He stood up and waved to my coach, who yelled back to him to stop by his casting office after lunch because he had a part for his daughter in one of his shows, and he did. That is how Hollywood worked back then.

My dad died on January 3, 1983. I was at the hospital with him every day, and the night before he went into a coma, he told that the chemo made him feel like his blood was on fire. The next day his body had metastasized with cancer, I was holding him in my arms and singing "Mack the Knife" when he took his last breath. I called my mom, who was at home with my son, and told her he was gone. The nurses all came in before I left and cried and told me how much they loved him. I kissed my dad goodbye and went home to take care of my mom and son.

My mom and I started to make arrangements for his funeral, and I called the head of casting and told him that my mom needed help to pay, as the costs at the hospital almost wiped them out. Universal started raising funds for his burial and chartered three buses from the studio to transport all of his friends to the funeral. So many people from all over Hollywood—writers, directors, producers, actors, agents, secretaries, assistants and casting directors and others—contributed to the fund for my dad's burial and attended his funeral. Over 350 people gathered at his grave site, and when they lowered my dad into the ground, I really felt like I was going to die right on the spot. I realized my life in Hollywood would never be the same again.

Ronald Reagan sent this lovely letter to my mom after his death:

The United States of America
Honors the memory of
Phil Benjamin
This certificate is awarded by a grateful

Nation in recognition of devoted and
Selfless consecration to the service
Of our country in the Armed Forces
Of the United States.

Ronald Reagan
President of the United States

Right after my dad's funeral, a producer friend of mine called me and said, "Hi kid, I have a job for you." This was back on the Universal lot, and I really didn't think I could walk on the lot again, but of course I did.

However, after that, there really wasn't that much work for me, and as much as I tried to take care of my mom, it just wasn't working out, because she didn't want to help take care of herself. My mom was so despondent and angry, and no matter how much I tried to help her, it just wasn't enough. It was so depressing to see her so unhappy day after day. She missed my dad so much.

My mom became friends with a woman who was the wife of our tax preparer. They were really awful to her, and I tried to tell her these people were not her friends. They kept asking her for money from my dad's life insurance policy and putting her in failing investments, even down to the man who installed her new carpets (and what an atrocious job the carpets were).

I couldn't do anything, so about a year later, I decided to take my son and go to Europe for a while. My mom dropped us off at the airport, and I would not return home for six years.

Shirley, Bobby, Lynn, Ray and Julia in CBS publicity shot for Hazel. *Photo courtesy CBS.*

Christmas family publicity shot for Hazel. *Photo courtesy CBS.*

Publicity photo of Bobby and Julia for Hazel. *Photo courtesy CBS.*

Backlot publicity shot of Lynn, Bobby, and Julia. Photo courtesy CBS.

Composite shot of Julia for interviews. Photo authors collection.

Valentines Day *TV show with Tony Franciosa and Julia. Photo authors collection.*

8x10 black and white publicity photo of Julia at 7 years old. Photo authors collection.

Julia's teacher, Catherine Deeney, and Julia, Stage 5, Hazel *set. Photo authors collection.*

Bobby, his mother, and Julia on Stage 5, Hazel *set. Photo authors collection.*

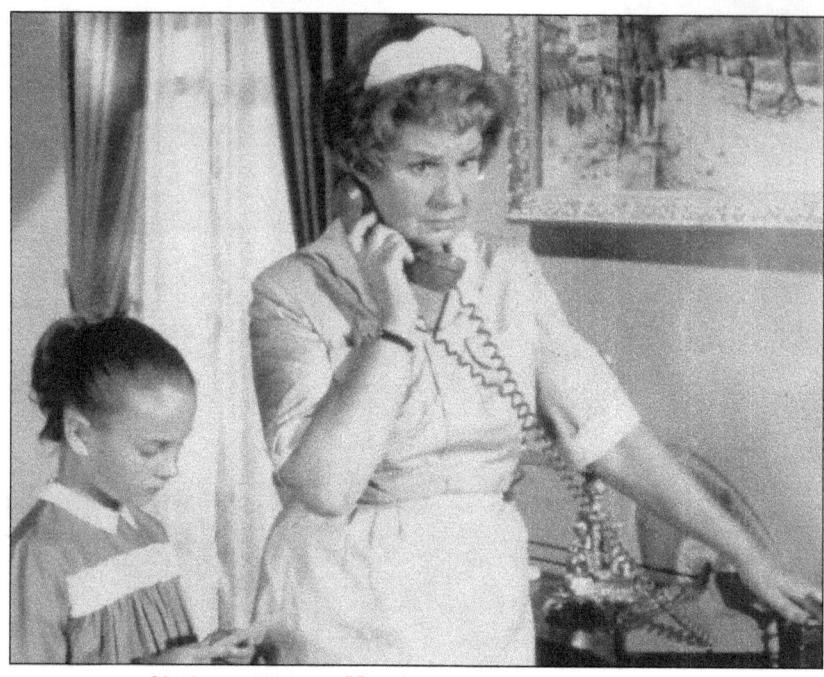

Shirley and Julia on Hazel *set. Photo courtesy collection.*

Hazel *Sound Director and Julia. Photo authors collection.*

Bobby at home with his homemade motor bike. Photo authors collection.

Bobby, Julia and Susie, Julia's new puppy from Bobby's poodle, in Bobby's living room. Photo authors collection.

Valentines Day *TV show, Tony's living room at the poker table. Julia at 7 years old, guest star, with Jack Soo and Tony. Photo authors collection.*

Julia's dressing room-trailer and chair, inside Stage 5. Photo authors collection.

In Hawaii with Gentle Ben the Bear, his trainer in the back with sunglasses on his shirt. Photo courtesy collection.

Juia's beagle Toddy and Julia, dressed in cowgirl suit, in her backyard in Granada Hills, California. Photo authors collection.

Dad and Julia cleaning their pool in Granada Hills. Photo authors collection.

TV Guide pictures from Hazel. Ray, Lynn, Bobby, Shirley and Julia on front lawn of backlot house. Julia is holding Petunia, her stuffed bulldog. Photo courtesy TV Guide.

TV guide article – Shirley with Ralph Bellamy at lunch, Shirley driving, Shirley in dressing room taking nap, and Shirley watching rushes (dailies). Photo courtesy TV Guide.

Hollywood Reporter article, CBS Hazel. *Authors collection.*

SHIRLEY BOOTH BAKER • 2276 BOWMONT DRIVE • BEVERLY HILLS, CALIFORNIA

June 12, 1965

Dear Julia:

Your lovely yellow roses faded on the last day I was in the hospital, but they were right by my bed for four whole lovely days and right now the beautiful receptacle they came in, is holding some artificial flowers to remind me of your kindness and thoughtfulness.

                Gratefully,

                Shirley Booth

sb;jfc

[Postmark: BEVERLY HILLS, JUN 12 PM 1965, CALIF.]

Julia Benjamin
c/o Screen Gems
1334 Beachwood Drive
Hollywood 28, Calif.

Letter from Shirley from the hospital on her stationary, showing her home address, after the show closed. Photo authors collection.

8x10 promotional photo of Julia at age 7, Jeanne Hallibourton Agency. Photo authors collection.

Julia 8x10. All famous children had their pictures taken by Amos Carr. He put them in the window on Hollywood Blvd. This picture showing "surprise" look. Photo authors collection.

Julia 8x10 by Amos Carr. This picture showing "angry" look. Photo authors collection.

Julia 8x10 by Amos Carr. This picture showing "sweet" look. Photo authors collection.

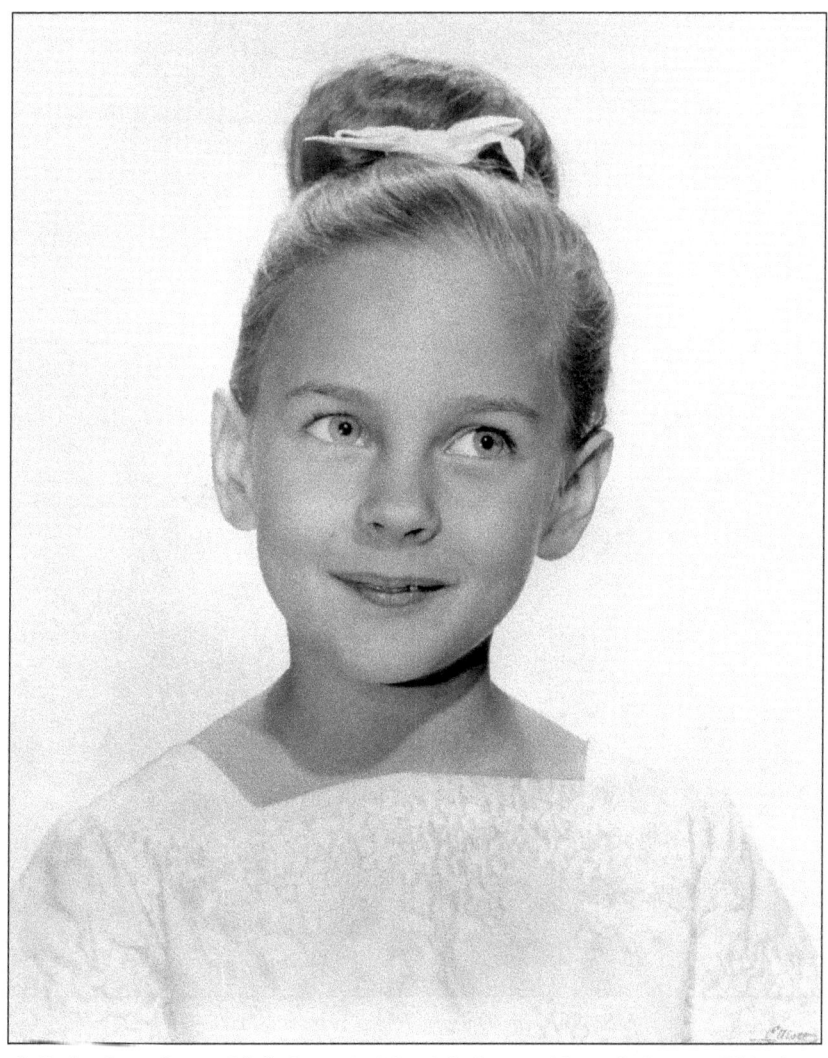

Julia by Amos Carr with "princess look" in pink dress and brocade flowers. This photo was used for the Marx Toys commercial. Photo authors collection.

Julia 8x10 at 10 years. Photo authors collection.

Julia 8x10 by Amos Carr at 9 years. Photo authors collection.

Julia 8x10 by Amos Carr. This picture showing "scarry" look. Photo authors collection.

Julia 8x10 by Amos Carr at 9 or 10 years old. Photo authors collection.

Julia 8x10 at 19 or 20 years old. Photo authors collection.

Julia's mother and father on the army base before they were married. Photo authors collection.

Julia's father on the army base in oversized uniform. Photo authors collection.

Julia's mother on the army base in uniform. Photo authors collection.

Julia's parents wedding picture. Photo authors collection.

Julia's parents wedding picture with family and friends. Photo authors collection.

Julia's mom singing with the troops and band for radio show. Photo authors collection.

Julia's mom as night club singer in Madison, Wisconson. Photo authors collection.

Julia's parents cutting the wedding cake and at the bar with army pals. Photo authors collection.

Julia's dad at studio, public relations. Photo authors collection.

Julia's parents in thier first apartment in Studio City after they were married. Photo authors collection.

Julia's grandmother with the racing form at her small San Fernando house. Photo authors collection.

Julia's dad on the phone, smoking a pipe, at Universal Sound Stage. Photo authors collection.

Julia's mom with Edith Head, famous wardrobe dresser, at the Motion Picture Television Luncheon in Beverly Hills. Photo includes Ann Doran and 2 other wives. Photo authors collection.

Julia's dad with studio heads on a casting call on the lot. Photo authors collection.

Julia's dad and all the studio gang at a evening gala, dressed up like all the current female movies stars. Photo authors collection.

Danny Kaye announcing at the studio gala. Photo authors collection.

Julia's dad with Johnny Grant, Mayor of Hollywood, and friends. Photo authors collection.

Julia's dad with famous babeball player and female star. Photo authors collection.

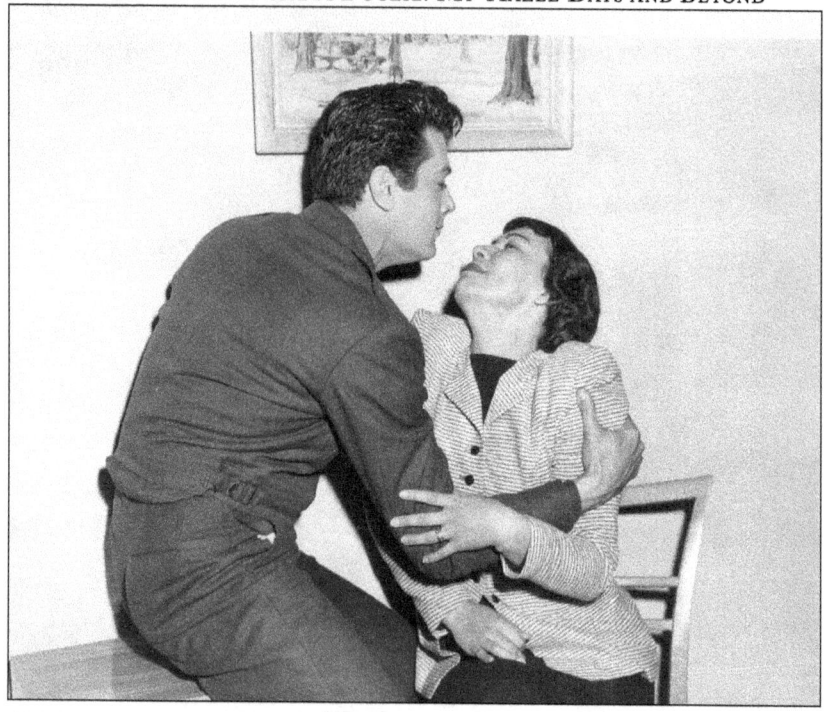

Julia's mom, hamming it up for publicty shot with Tony Curtis. Photo authors collection.

Julia's mom and Tony Curtis exchange money for war bonds. Photo authors collection.

Julia's dad on the cover of a casting magazine. Photo authors collection.

The United States of America honors the memory of

PHIL BENJAMIN

This certificate is awarded by a grateful nation in recognition of devoted and selfless consecration to the service of our country in the Armed Forces of the United States.

Ronald Reagan
President of the United States

Julia's father is honored by President Ronald Reagan. Photo authors collection.

The gang at Camp Hann for their show. Photo authors collection.

Julia's Aunt Izzy and Lou Costello. Photo authors collection.

CHAPTER 11 – MY BIG FAT GREEK SABBATICAL

It was great when we arrived in Greece. I chose Greece because of the return of the dollar to the drachma. We took a flat in Kolonaki, and I enrolled my son in a private pre-school in Pangrati called Stepping Stones. It was wonderful, as English ladies ran it, so every morning, I would walk Branden over to the English Embassy from our nearby flat, and a taxi would take him with a few other children to his nursery school. I would continue and work in Greece's entertainment industry. They loved blue-eyed blondes, so getting work to add to my residuals that were coming in was easy. We stayed there for a year before we moved to the American community base of Glyfada by the sea. Branden went to another English school called Peter Pan, again where he was picked up by a small bus and delivered back to me in the early afternoon.

While I was working and taking care of my son, a Greek actor/diplomat who knew my father invited me to have a coffee with him. As we were having coffee, I realized that he was the most arrogant, chauvinistic man I think I have ever known. Still, he insisted that I meet a couple of his friends to have a social life while we were there. One of his friends would not stop calling me, a little short man who claimed he was an executive consultant for the ship owners and worked for one of the international papers. At first he was very nice, but when I found out he was married, I asked him not to call me again. Unfortunately, I was so naïve that I gave in and started to date him. He was very nice to my child, but he had insatiable sexual problems. Yet he always lured me into his world of travel and elite crowds of people and exclusive events in Greece or around Europe.

I continued doing some print work and commercials, and at one point I had a billboard up all around Greece for a fabric softener holding a baby. Then we did a lot of traveling and about twenty cruises with my son. I already did my first cruise in Greece with my son before I met this man, a day trip to the three islands. My favorite of all three on this day trip was Hydra, very close to Athens. The reason I loved it so much is because when the ship comes in to debark, so many cats, all different colors and sizes, are waiting too on the little dock to greet you upon arrival.

With my male companion, my son and I cruised to so many of the Greek islands, each so very beautiful and unique—Mykonos, Rhodes, Crete, Santorini, Corfu, the list goes on and on. We learned about the history of the Greeks and the Romans, which is so fascinating. I always stopped at each island to walk into all the many churches, which are so beautiful and fascinating, especially those from the Byzantine era. When we were not cruising, I traveled to London, Italy, France, Switzerland and several times to Turkey.

Branden and I stayed in Greece for six years until I decided that it was time to go home. I really was so unhappy the way this man started in the end to treat me as well, so controlling, jealous, and sexually abusive. The upside was that almost every day in the evenings, my son and I would go to his office when everyone had left and call my mom to see how she was doing. I would let her know that I had a package of gifts on the way to her from wherever I had just traveled to, but nothing I did seemed to make her happy.

It took about six weeks to get ready to come home, but finally we did. We left and arrived in New York City. While we were in Greece, a lovely Greek American woman who was in advertising had an apartment in New York where she let us stay in her place while I managed all her day-to-day affairs. The apartment, located on the east side in Sutton Place between First Avenue and the East River, was just beautiful. The guy from Greece came without warning a few times there too, but finally it ended, thank God.

CHAPTER 12 – Big Mistake in the Big Apple

I enrolled Branden, now seven years old, in school and got an agent to continue my acting and voice career in New York City for the next three years. The first six months in New York were very hard to get used to. I love the Big Apple, but it will wear you down. Once I started landing commercials and voiceovers, it was great.

Towards the last six months in New York, I was working in a post-production studio for two really nice producers who would let me go out on interviews when my agent called while I worked for them. I learned a lot about how the producers shoot on location in New York with permits and deadlines. I was lucky and landed a nice voiceover and some commercials for a steakhouse and an eye glass company that kept us going. I decided since I now knew all the advertisers, producers and casting directors that Branden and I would head back home to Los Angeles and go back to work in Hollywood.

Just as I was starting to plan to go home, walking on 57th Street and Second Avenue to pick up my son from the bus stop where his school, Saint Ignatius Loyola, dropped off all the kids, I walked past the very famous comedian I mentioned earlier, and we said hello. He invited me to his partner and co-star's theater group for the opening. I had a great time, but that crazed actress who knew him and my dad called me as the comedian gave her my phone number. Still, things were going really good for my son and myself, and we were excited to come home and see my mom and get back to work in Hollywood.

But while I was working at the production office, and shortly after my evening out with the comedian, a man that knew one of the producer/owners where I was working was calling one of my bosses every day. Then he started calling me all day long at work, every day for a couple of weeks. Eventually I told him if he would stop calling me while I was working, I would give him my home phone number and we could talk after I was finished helping my son with his homework and getting him into bed and ready for school the next day.

What the hell was I thinking? Anyway I gave him my number and he called me that evening. We talked for about an hour. He said he wanted to fly in from Florida to New York for the weekend to see his mom and stepfather in New Jersey. When he arrived in town, he invited Branden and me to drive with him to visit with his mom and stepdad. Since he knew my boss, I thought this was OK and might be fun, so we drove to New Jersey, then had dinner that night back in the city in Little Italy.

He asked me if he could sleep over that night. Like a fool, I said yes. I was so naïve then; I have no idea why I said yes. I was on the A list in New York with advertisers, producers and casting directors on a request basis. I had just had a power lunch with one of the top agents in New York and was very close to making it big again in the entertainment industry. I had a plan to come back to Los Angeles to see my mom, and since I had already met all the top advertisers, I was ready to really get back to work.

Still, as soon as we all were ready for bed, he asked me to marry him. He said he was a Top Gun, a lawyer in an aviation office and a FBI agent. Oh, Julia. Why I said yes after being asked to get married seven times, I'll never know, except he was such a con artist, he believed his own lies too, and I fell victim to him.

I called my mom to tell her about this man, but when I spoke to my sister, she put a woman on the phone that clearly was not my mother, I called back the next day and told my sister if she did not put my mom on the phone, I would call the police. My mom picked up the phone a few minutes later, and here's the conversation we had.

"Mom, how are you doing?"
"Fine."
"Do you have your add-on built yet?"
"Yes."
"Is everyone being good to you?"
"When are you coming home?"
"I'd like to soon, mom. Where shall we all go? You Branden and me?"

"Well, you've got a point."

"I'm coming home, Mom, and we'll figure this whole mess out. Your son-in-law called me after I told you about this man who asked me to marry him."

"Really?"

"Yes, your son-in-law wants to put you in a home."

"Does he? It doesn't surprise me."

"I'm coming home, Mom, I love you."

"I love you too, Julia. Bye."

In a matter of weeks, I was married to this man at the United Nations chapel in New York City. We packed up his rented car with all of our belongings, and I took the worst drive of my life back to his house in Florida. The whole way, he was so angry, furious, and driving unheard of speeds back. My son and I were terrified.

Here is where my nightmare started. When we arrived, he lived in the worst part in Hollywood, Florida, certainly not the picture he painted. I kept asking him what was wrong, but he kept telling me that I knew. I had no idea.

So the next morning I enrolled my son in a nearby school and started to clean up his dump of a house. I knew I'd better do something quickly. I went out to see the agents in Florida to introduce myself and start going on interviews. He had no job, no money and by the pill boxes in his refrigerator that I cleaned out—Halcyon, Prozac and other mind-altering drugs—I knew he was nuts.

The washer didn't work. He was blaming my son and me because the plumbing always broke. You couldn't even walk into the kitchen at night because the roaches would come out from everywhere. The neighbor next to us had a pig, the ones behind us owned ferrets and the man a few houses down would ride his swamp boat on his front lawn.

Once he brought home some kind of a telephone transmitter he claimed he got from the FBI that he used to dial in and listen to the neighbor's telephone calls. Another day, he left his bedroom desk drawer open, and I saw it was filled with names and pictures of him with different eye colors and hair colors. There were several various Social Security numbers and drivers' licenses too.

Creditors called the house morning noon and night. He demanded that I sign my name to many of his credit cards. If not, he threatened to harm both my son and me. And guess who was calling his house all the time? That crazy actress from Hollywood. Many times she called and only spoke with him, and I had no idea.

I was getting ready to get on a bus with my son and come back to California. But one Friday, I went on an interview for a pasta sauce commercial and got an appointment to come back in that Monday to meet with the advertisers, I knew the casting director, a great gal, and it looked like they were going to pick me. So I would shoot that and get away from this guy as soon as my first paycheck came in. Fate had other plans for me.

CHAPTER 13 – THE ATTACK AND THE AFTERMATH

That Sunday was Valentine's Day. The three of us had gone shopping earlier that morning, and he said he wanted to take my son out for a few hours to do guy stuff while I started to prepare a barbecue dinner. We bought shrimp, steaks, a red and white iced heart shaped cake for dessert, everything we needed to have a wonderful dinner that evening. I was so happy and excited for my callback the next morning too.

Buckle up folks. Here's where I'm married to Norman Bates and run into Cujo.

I walked outside the back door of the house to start the barbecue. Unbeknownst to me, the dog next door, an Akita, had gotten out of the backyard from a ten-foot chained link fence, and the owners were gone. Supposedly the dog chewed a hole in the fence and was roaming freely in the neighborhood. The ex even told me this was a vicious dog earlier, and I asked him to make a phone call to have the dog either picked up or call the owners and let them know, as there were a lot of small children in the neighborhood playing outside, but he didn't.

I sat down to smoke a cigarette. I never smoked inside the house or my ex would go into a rage. (In fact, he was always in a rage, but he seemed very calm and happy that day, almost likable.) The dog came around the side of the house and sat down right by my feet.

I started to get up to go back into the house, and the dog lunged at my left breast, completely ripping it off, then lunged at my left arm and dragged me twenty-five feet into the bushes. He was shaking me so hard I felt like a rag doll, and I was bleeding badly from my breast and arm. He kept pulling and snarling and had just about pulled off my left arm. This lasted for about twenty minutes while I was on the ground, flat on my back in the bushes, before I finally screamed "Daddy, help me!" because I was almost passing out. The sky above me was starting to open up, and while I was trying to kick the dog in the groin, he was humping me at the same time.

The girl in the house behind ours heard me scream and called 911. The next door neighbor on the other side of the dog came out with a gun, while the man who rode his swamp boat started hitting the dog as hard as he could on his back with a short steel pipe bar. The man was very tall and supposedly an ex-Navy SEAL officer, and he yelled at me to stay still when finally the dog let me go to lunge at him instead.

The minute the dog let go, I held on to my left arm and got up and went back into the house. I walked out at three o'clock and went back inside at three twenty five. I stood in the kitchen, and all I wanted to do was take a shower to get the smell off of me. I could hardly move, I couldn't talk, and I walked over to the living room window ledge and sat down.

Suddenly from every direction, people started coming in from the front and back doors of the house—police, neighbors, and people I didn't know until the ambulance driver came in with bandages. By that time I was hysterical. I was bleeding badly and didn't want anyone to touch me. I was shaking so hard, and I was scared. The paramedics started to cut off my pink blouse, and there were so many people standing there watching. Their faces were looking at me with horrified expressions of what a mess I was.

By the time they were ready to move me to the ambulance outside, the SWAT team was on the roof with shotguns. I remember putting my right arm over my face so no one could look at me.

The ride was so hard, each bump made me scream with pain. On the way to the hospital, I could hear the ambulance driver dispatching my size, weight and hair color and that I had partial balding in the front of my head where the trees had ripped out so much of my hair. Midway to the hospital, the dispatcher from Memorial East told them to go to Memorial West, as the plastic surgeon would not be available. I don't remember getting the rest of the way to the hospital, maybe I passed out, I don't know.

I just remember being in the emergency room for a long time and wondering where my son and soon-to-be-estranged husband were. Amid all the pain, I was thinking to myself why he hadn't called all day when he called every day all day long and especially if my baby boy was OK. It was strange that in the eight months we had been married, this guy never left to go anywhere for very long, but on this day he decided to take my son and go fishing in the Everglades—no phone, no beeper, no calls. He knew we were going to have a barbecue in the afternoon for Valentine's Day dinner; we had gone to the store in the morning. He even knew that the dog had attacked a woman three years earlier, but he made no calls to have the dog picked up that day.

While I was in the hospital, the woman who had been attacked by the same dog came to see me unannounced and said the dog had jumped up and dragged her into the middle of the street by the back of her neck. When she took the owners to court, they laughed at her, and when they walked by her and her husband, the owners said, "Woof woof!"

I waited and waited before I would go into surgery to see if my son was on the way until finally the doctor came in, a plastic surgeon so kind and gentle. He asked me for my name and Social Security number and other questions and told me that it was crucial that I go into surgery for irrigation and of course stitches. A lot of stitches.

My son and ex never showed up as I was finally taken to the first operation to be irrigated and cleaned up. When I awoke, my son and ex had finally arrived at the hospital, but the doctor told me that my ex could see me but not my son. I told the doctor that I had only been married for a few months and I have never been away from my son as a single parent or my son away from me, so he brought my son to me immediately.

I will never forget the look on Branden's face, I told him I was going to be OK, but I really wasn't sure, and I was afraid I was going to lose my left arm. My son told me later he never saw anyone hooked up to so many machines in his life, not even on TV. As I was wheeled down to my room where I would stay for twelve days, my son and ex were there waiting for me. My son started to cry, but the ex looked almost elated and grinned from ear to ear, almost like at this point he saw money.

They didn't stay very long, and I couldn't sleep at all that night. I kept hearing someone walking up and down the corridor hall with keys, and it terrified me as it sounded like the chain of the dog. I was put on a morphine machine where you pushed the button every time the pain would be unbearable. I was scared, sick and in pain. A lot of pain.

The next morning, a great gal, a nurse came in while I was in the bathroom. I was going to take a shower no matter what, I couldn't stand the smell of the dog on me, and the dirt was so far embedded under my nails I couldn't believe it. As I waited in the bathroom, my nurse went to go get plastic wrap and tape, and we closed the door and washed me from head to toe, even my hair with the small hand soap. It was very painful to wash then and sometimes even now.

Just as I got back into bed, the soon-to-be-ex came into the room unannounced in a suit followed by a camera crew from a local television station. I started to cry and begged him not to do this to me, but he carried on with the camera interview anyway. He was so happy it was sickening, and he loved to be in front, behind or anywhere near the camera acting like a famous producer.

He also came back at five o'clock to show me the interview that was on television that evening, laughing and asking me did I think he looked good. I was so upset, I felt like a human spectacle, and he was so pleased with himself.

The upside was that the neighbors made sure my son came up to see me every day after school. We'd watch cartoons together, and I had him right next to me in my bed until he had to leave. I should have insisted that a cot be brought in for him to stay by my side, as I'll soon explain.

By Day Three I was back down in surgery again for four hours, with more irrigation all day long and stitches and four million units of antibiotics every four hours. I was a wreck, with more camera crews and interviews with people showing up. My phone never stopped ringing, and it was hard to answer with one arm.

Even with the surgeries, it hurt so badly on my raw skin when I felt the air after the bandages were changed. The morphine numbed the pain, but it made me feel sick. There were two germs from the dog living inside of me that could not be killed. I still had not eaten, because I couldn't open the plastic wrap covering the knife and fork. Also, I was too embarrassed to ask for help.

Day Four had still too many people and too many calls, and that actress from Los Angeles purposely called every half hour or so, knowing that I couldn't pick up the phone. What a bunch of crap. I was supposed to go down to surgery again, but I drank some water and they brought me back to my room. Meanwhile, the ex totally exploited me by taking the money from all the interviews with *The National Enquirer, Star, Hard Copy* and all the other media he contacted.

On Day Five, I was scheduled for surgery at 6 a.m. I asked the soon-to-be ex to please come in the morning and wait with me. I was scared, and I didn't want to be alone. It was hard to get him to come, and he didn't feel like waiting around while I was being prepped again because he said he was too busy. I didn't understand.

That evening, the doctor came in to irrigate me again. He still can't kill the germs living inside of me, and I can't stop crying and I don't know why. But the doctor did have all the phone calls and visitors stopped. Thank you.

Day 10 on a Wednesday evening, the ex arrived with my son. During a conversation we had about how he was planning to make a movie about my tragic accident, he grabbed my foot. This scared me so much that I jumped out of bed and got caught up in the hospital curtain, tearing the stitches in my arm that the dog nearly severed. The nurse called my doctor, and I told him the ex refused to take care of my son. Since the doctor saw my son come up every day, he insisted that my child stay with me that evening.

A day or two before I was to be released from the hospital, a psychiatrist was scheduled to come in and see me. That only made me angrier than I already was. He was a young man, about thirty, and when he came into talk with me, I hardly said a word. When I did speak with him, it had nothing to do with the dog attack.

I was really concerned about being in an abusive relationship and having my son stuck with this maniac without me to watch him. I knew no matter how I felt that I needed to get out of the hospital for the sake of Branden. My baby's eyes had dark circles under them, something had happened to him, and I knew I had to protect him.

The evening before I was to be released from the hospital, the ex came in with a man who supposedly was the head of an aviation firm that he supposedly worked for. They told me that they were both going to represent me with the dog attack. Out of $100,000 from the next door neighbors' title insurance, they wanted $15,000. I was forced by the ex to sign off on papers even though I didn't know what they were.

At this point, I really knew something was up. I was still so sick, and what the hell was the big hurry? I wasn't even out of the hospital yet, and again the ex flew into another rage when I started to ask questions about the insurance money and the paperwork he was shoving under my face to sign without reading.

The next day I was released from the hospital, and while the ex was waiting for my release papers, he was angry and in a rage again. What a lunatic. The greed on his face made him look contorted. It took about two hours for the hospital to release me—a very long two hours. On the drive home to his house, he did not say one word to me.

When we did finally get back home, it was a mess, looking as though he had had a party while I was in the hospital for the twelve days. On Valentine's Day, the day of the dog attack, the house was in stellar condition. Now it was a mess, with booze bottles and food on the counters. The floors were dirty and all sticky, certainly not the way I left it even with the dog attack.

About two days after I got home, the ex arranged for the insurance people to come by for an interview prior to the settlement. The male Akita dog that attacked me was gone, but the female was still there, and she had just given birth to five little puppies while I was in the hospital. Now there were six dogs next door, and they just cried and yelped all day and night long. Before the male Akita attacked me, his hair was falling out in clumps. It really was a hideous sight, and he used to jump on the female and bite and tear her neck until she was bleeding.

On the day the insurance adjusters were to arrive at 11 a.m., I had a hard time getting dressed. The ex started coaching me about what to say. I thought that the truth was horrific enough—what prompting needed to be said?

The insurance settlement money was $100,000. However, the ex and his so-called boss of the aviation firm were in such a hurry to get the money that a great deal of the settlement was spent immediately on lawyers' fees, the hospital, two plastic surgeons, therapists, MRIs and two anesthesiologists for each of the four surgeries.

The ex insisted that I deposit $7,000 into our joint account. I kept $3,000 and used $1,500 to close out my New York apartment in arrears ten months later, as the ex didn't have a job when we got married. He had totally misrepresented himself, telling me, "Marry me and fly for free, lover, and you'll be wearing diamonds bigger than horse turds. I have five corporations, work if you want and let's have another child." None of which was true, and thank God I didn't bring another demon child with his blood into this world. God was truly looking after my son and me.

Instead of paying the bills or house payment he owed, the ex took the first $100 in the account and bought a rifle and a handgun along with a compound bow for my son. I couldn't believe it. Next he started to bring home manuals for utility vehicles starting at $26,000.

Sadly over the next couple of days, all the dogs next door were destroyed, even the puppies. Proudly, the ex said he was the reason why. He destroyed everything he came in contact with—when we left New York, Branden and I had a little Betta fish that we took with us on the drive to Florida, and the ex took it out of the water and put it in a plastic baggie while we both watched as he let it suffocate and flop around on the sink. He said it because it was sick and needed to die.

The day after the insurance people came, I was sitting on the bed and the ex started hitting me in the head when my child came into the room. Branden asked the ex why he was doing that and to stop.

I did go out and buy a small used car for about $3,000 with cash. That would provide a way for my son and me to get the hell away from him. I had to do that because my ex refused to take me to therapy for my rehabilitation for my arm, which I had to stop too.

One of his sicker moments—and there were a lot—was while I was wrapped in bandages and would try to rest in bed or while we were sleeping, he would take his hand and wipe his own excrement on the bedsheets.

And the one and only time he took my son to school in the morning in his truck, he pulled over and pulled out a plastic bag he had under his driver's seat. It was the pink blouse that I had been attacked in with the dog, and he started to smell the blouse and laugh. Then told my son to smell it too.

Given these instances, on the weekends for a short time, I drove with my son to Naples, Florida, just to get away from the ex. But he arrived on the third trip, more angry and violent. Nothing ever changed with him, he was so dysfunctional and such a sick person.

He never stopped blaming us for everything that had gone wrong in his life. I had asked him very early on why he had no relations with his two grown children, and he started punching my arm. He knocked me off my feet two times after cornering me in the kitchen just prior to the dog attack.

Another time I went to look for my son and found out that my ex had grabbed Branden by the arm and took him outside and was punching my son in the arm too. The neighbors that lived behind us told me that he had coldcocked his last wife while she was sleeping in bed, because she supposedly was having an affair, or so he thought. By then, I realized we had to get out of there soon.

Just before we were ready to leave, the ex demanded more money, so I gave him another $3,000. Even his sisters called or came over and demanded that I give them money, and he said he was going to take my child away from me and put me in an insane asylum.

Right before we left to start our journey home to California, the ex took the car I had just bought and said he wanted to check it out. What we found out on the drive home is that he had placed a roach nest underneath the dashboard of the windshield, and the roaches on the drive back home started coming out everywhere whenever we had any food or snacks for the drive.

My son and I have often wondered through the years, especially when he got rid of the nurse that would come by the house to change the dressings, why a representative from the hospital didn't come by and speak with me directly or my son, or why someone from the state of Florida didn't come by and ask me what had happened. The reason is that quite frankly he had alienated us from everyone, everywhere.

CHAPTER 14 – CORRESPONDENCE CHAOS

Here begins the paper trail from hell. I can't say enough how badly I want the ex to leave me alone. I was sick, and sick of him, utterly disgusted.

The aviation lawyer wrote the first letter on March 26, 1993 and let the ex and I know how pleased he was that the bank cleared the check for $100,000 which is now available. He also has received the bills for expenses from the two doctors, the surgeon and the psychiatrist. Here is the breakdown:

15% of attorneys fee—$15,000
Expenses—$79.15
Hospital lien—$19,592.50
Loan to client—$100
Broadcast Quality—$48.35
Surgeon—$4,670
Psychiatrist—$605

That comes to a total of $40,095, leaving a net recovery of $59,905. Of that, the ex and the aviation lawyer took $10,000, leaving a balance of remaining funds at $49,905. And the $49,905 is supposedly for the rest of my life to recover, but all the money is spent instead by me defending myself through this divorce.

On the same day the aviation lawyer wrote a letter to the surgeon and agrees to pay him the $4,670 with his Trust Account check for the following:

02/14/93 DEBRIDEMENT of Arm $140
02/14/93 DEBRIDEMENT Skin $275
02/14/93 Emergency consultation $150
02/17/93 DEBRIDEMENT ABRASION $95
02/20/93 COMPLEX REPAIR of BREAST $2,000
02/23/93 COMPLEX REPAIR UPPER ARM $2,000

Also on the same day, the aviation lawyer wrote a letter to the psychiatrist and agreed to pay him the $605 with his Trust Account check. If any further treatment or consultations of service were needed, the psychiatrist was instructed to send the bill to me, Julia.

Of course, no one ever discussed anything with me to approve or disapprove with this accident. Incidentally, I have no idea who or what Broadcast Quality was for in the amount of $48.35.

With this it's time to hit the road and head back home while I still have any money left at all. Branden and I left with our little used car and headed up north. We stopped in to see a friend of my dad's who was now the head of casting at Universal Florida. He used to be my dad's assistant, and I knew I could trust him. Realizing I had a huge problem, he directed us on a completely different route to get home—Interstate 10 West all the way. I had packed two suitcases but also had my things picked up by UPS and shipped by ground to an apartment in Marina Del Rey.

We arrived in Los Angeles May 17, 1993, and immediately the leasing agent told me that the ex had put out a missing person's report. We arrived to many Western Union Mailgrams and handwritten letters including threats from my ex too. Even a woman from the Los Angeles County Department of Child Services claimed there was an anonymous report of child abuse with my son.

Deputies with the sheriff's department also came by three times upon our arrival home. First the leasing agent told them there was no foul play, the next time they were asking me to come downstairs to discuss the alleged foul play, and finally they came by on a report that I was going to commit suicide. On the third time, the deputies came by that evening because the ex was spotted hanging out by the Jacuzzi by the security guards in the building, and the police came by again that night to check as well. I also met the host of the *Hard Copy* segment, which was filmed in Florida.

Here is the ex's first handwritten letter, dated May 20, 1993:

Julia,

This is to advise you that since you have failed to contact me on arrival in California as we agreed before you left, and you have failed to wire the $5,000 which you promised, I have no reason to believe that you wish to remain married, so therefore I have instructed my attorney to file for divorce and ask for half of all the insurance settlement we received as a result of the February 14, 1993 dog attack, plus on the properties and money. We have been in contact with an attorney from L.A. who advise us any judgment gotten in Florida can be enforced in California. I am enclosing a copy of the release that shows I'm entitled to half.

I did fail to contact this monster. We came home to get away from him and get a divorce. He referred to the dog attack as "we," meaning him, and every letter and mailgram referred to money. I'm writing these letters just the way he wrote them, and believe me, I never promised him anything more, I just wanted to get away from him.

Mailgram dated May 26, 1993:

Julia,

Because you failed to wire the $5,000, I cannot get to California to my new job in time. So therefore it looks as though I won't be coming out to California. Thanks for being there when I needed help. I should have known I couldn't count on you.

I was served with a summons for a legal separation and restraining order, had many personal letters from the ex saying the house in Florida are his and that he will endeavor to take half of all my insurance settlement money as well as all my expenditures including my car and income tax and employment earnings in a slander suit.

Next, I received a letter from the aviation lawyer, who said that while the ex and I are looking for a reduction in the $19,592.50 hospital bill, interest will accrue. He asked if I would prefer to endorse the check and send it back to Florida to deliver to the hospital and noted that since I moved, the lawyer will not continue to hold the check while the ex and I explore more options.

I never asked the ex at any time to explore options with the check. I thought it was already sent to the hospital, and the ex and I had not spoken one word since I got home. Now I'm starting to wonder about paying this bill to the hospital, and there's always this "we" thing going on.

It takes months before this check makes it over to the hospital. Also, the ex is in debt to everyone. Here's the next mailgram, dated May 27, 1993.

RE: account xxxxxx

Imperative we have $565.79 in our office no later than Saturday, May 29 or we will have no choice but to take legal action. Please govern yourself accordingly.

Associates Financial Services.

Of course I have no idea what this is.
Next mailgram, May 29, 1993, from the ex:

Dear Julia,

Please call me. Your broken promise created big problems down at this end, or don't you care? Remember I'm still your husband.

This paper trail shows the harassment he sent during this time. His handwritten letter dated June 1, 1993 shows his bizarre behavior, including references to his "committee in my mind." There was never any correspondence from me personally to him at all. None.

Dear Julia,

I guess I should start this letter by saying I love you. The past few weeks have not been easy. As I'm sure, your time has not been easy either. This letter is one of the few times I will put anything in black and white that comes from my heart.

In less than two weeks our first anniversary will be here, and we are apart, telling friends and family we want a divorce and doing what we can to hurt each other, because we feel we've been hurt by the other person. A year ago we heard each other choose and make special promises to each other which we hoped would last a lifetime. But now we sit on the brink of what we both hoped would never happen. The end of our marriage.

It now seems that neither of us want to pull back, because we're afraid it will show a sign of weakness. Two weeks ago, I wrote you a letter saying that I was filing for a divorce and wanted half of the insurance money and everything else. After I sent the letter, I realized maybe it wasn't a good idea. I'm sure some things you've done over the last few weeks might seem like not a good idea either.

But now comes the time to put our anger and egos in check and question whether we really want the marriage to end. We need to talk out what's bothering us and see if we can't give a little bit more of ourselves to each other before we lose what we both wanted and have worked so hard for.

The first year of marriage has not been easy for us, and of all the things that have happened, you have suffered the worst damage of all. Maybe I needed to hold you and hug you a little more and say I love you just a bit more than normal, but sometimes I felt I need just a little bit more from you. And maybe I should have said something. But as you well know, my little committee upstairs doesn't always feel like letting people know what's going on inside me, and maybe the time has come to replace this committee with a committee of one—my wife.

So here goes the first opening gesture. I have not and will not file for a divorce, because as much as I hate to admit it, I really do love you. If you really do want a divorce, then you'll have to be the one to file. As for the insurance money that always been yours, all I wanted before you left was enough to help me get started when I got to California, so we would have a steady income while you recovered and decided what you wanted to do with your career. You would have gotten you money back tenfold, because the job that await me is pretty great. But now that all on hold.

I've always make a point to do what's best for you and never really wanted anything in return. Now you have the power to do what you think is right. So use your power wisely, because what decision you make will affect all of us for a lifetime.

But remember I will always love you.

The ex just can't stop. There was never any love from him, and that's my fault. He wanted money, period, and he didn't care how he got it or who he took down getting it. He had never been to California before he met me.

Another mailgram, June 4, 1993:

Dear Julia,

I'll be in L.A. this weekend. If you want to pick me up at the airport, let me know. Otherwise, I'll see you when I get there.

Next mailgram, June 7, 1993:

Dear Julia,

I will be staying in Marina Del Rey at the Foghorn Hotel until we have our problems resolved. I now have an attorney who is ready to file the appropriate paperwork for me to recover the amount of money that I seek. This letter is a last offer to resolve our problems in a friendly manner.

Under California law, I am entitled to one half of everything acquired after we were married (including your car). This letter should arrive approximately around noon to one o'clock on June 8, 1993. If I do not hear from you by 3:30 in the afternoon with an amicable resolution to our problems, I will file for legal separation, and you could lose half of real and personal property and monies that you have acquired during our marriage.

I still love you. We have an anniversary Sunday. Let's let us try to rebuild instead of destroy. But be advised I'm ready to go to the mat, and California law is on my side.

I Love You

I have never been around a person so vicious in my life. Again, this is all about money. Never once does he ask if I'm OK, only what he thinks he's entitled to or what he is going to take, and still not one bit of communication back from me. Nothing.

Another mailgram, no date:

Julia,

I'm in town, call me in room 110.

This is the same room my son and I stayed in when we arrived back in Los Angeles waiting for our apartment to be ready. The ex is such a freak, and it's becoming clear to me that the actress from the past is very much in the background.

Mailgram, no date:

Dear Julia,

I'm sorry about last night. Let's try to resolve things. Please. I'm staying one more night, please call me. We love each other. Let's try to work something out before we send each other to the funny farm.

Your part-time husband.

When the ex wrote from the motel that he is sorry about last night, it was the only time I saw him through the advice of "friends" to try to reconcile. This was a huge mistake. My son was staying with a friend. I drove to the little motel to pick up the ex, and we drove down Pacific Avenue off of Washington at the beach. He pulled the keys from the car's ignition, jumped out and ran across the street laughing while he's dangling the keys at me. Everyone on Pacific had to stop as my car was stopped in the middle of the street, until a couple of guys in trucks saw what had happened. They were angry and jumped out of their trucks and made sure my ex gave me back my keys so I could move the car out of the street. The ex jumped back in the car, and we left.

The ex loved being a bully every chance he got. I dropped him back off at the motel. He had a truck that was paid for but still he wanted the little subcompact I bought for $3,000 with taxes and registration out the door.

CHAPTER 15 – MORE LETTERS, MORE LAWYERS

While I was in the hospital, the ex had taken my day timer with all my contacts and numbers, and he started calling everyone during the divorce. He was going around Hollywood with pictures of my breast and arm, trying to sell my story for money. He even told everyone he had known my dad for years. More lies.

During a protective hearing, while we were in the courtroom and I was on the stand, I told the female judge that my left arm and left breast was an intimate and personal part of my female anatomy and asked to make this man stop humiliating me in my hometown. I was awarded the rights to my story and protective orders against.

Now we're home, but I'm still getting so much harassing mail from the ex that I knew it was time to get a lawyer. I decided to give a call to the host of the TV series *Hard Copy*. She had called me while I was in the hospital and gave me her direct line to call her as soon as we got back to Los Angeles. What a great help she was to me.

She introduced my son and myself to her anchor. He called me and introduced himself to me, then asked me if I saw the previous segment of my dog attack on *Hard Copy*. The ex insisted that we watch this at 2 a.m. in Florida when it aired. I told him I did but I was so sick I really didn't remember. Next he asked me if I ever watched the show, and I told him no. He started laughing and I asked him why. He told me that was good because that meant I had a life.

The next thing he asked me if I saw the man sitting next to his co-host. Again I said no, but finally I realized who he was. It was really embarrassing, because when we met, he took Branden and me out for dinner, and everyone knew who he was. He was so kind to my son and me, because no one would talk to me that I knew, and when I tell you no one, I mean no one. People I had known for years wouldn't even speak with me, and to this day I still don't know what my horrible ex said to everyone.

You find out quickly who your friends are when a tragedy happens. The host of the show couldn't have been more of a godsend. My son and he spent so much time together, going out for burgers and shakes and the movies, and he even brought home make up from the studio for my son for Halloween.

Both hosts knew and understood the ex's bizarre behavior because the ex had called and harassed them all day long. The female host was so kind and a great girlfriend. She understood my situation and set me up with her hairdresser in Beverly Hills, who was just wonderful. I was finally able to get my hair done, and the gal that cut my hair helped me get my gown on because I was in a lot of pain.

Next I went to see a lawyer I had worked for during hiatus one year when Branden was about nine months old just to make a little extra cash. He referred me to two different lawyers. I met them both, the first one in Century City and the second one in Laguna Beach. As I look back, I should have taken the lawyer in Century City because I would have had my divorce much sooner, and he would have never put up with all the antics of the ex. They both wanted $5,000 to start, but they were different as night and day. When you feel so sick and your being harassed constantly and threatened you do the best you can.

A certified mail with return receipt requested arrived June 11, 1993. It read:

Dear Julia,

On June 9, 1993, you were served with a Summons for Legal Separation. This Letter is a follow-up request with regard to the Summons and Restraining Order. I hereby request the following:

1. A detailed account of all money expended prior to and after leaving Florida May 7, 1993.

2. Current balance on any and all account including checking, savings, money market and other accounts which you now hold or are a signatory or trustee of fiduciary or have held.

3. A detailed list of "all expenditures" including furniture, household appliances, and personal items purchased after leaving Florida on May 7, 1993.

4. A copy of our joint 1992 Income Tax Returns for review before signature is affixed and sent to the IRS for anticipated $1,200 refund.

5. Full disclosure of your employment earnings/salary as stated by you on June 5, 1993.

6. Cease and desist unsubstantiated allegations as to my character and behavior: libel and slander.

If you make any extraordinary expenditure, I must be notified five days in advance as per the Restraining Order, and also to advise you of any of my expenditures. Please direct all future communications and correspondence to the above address, including you attorney's name, address and telephone number.

Next mailgram, June 15, 1993:

Dear Julia,

The address for response to request in the June 11, 1993 letter was incorrect. The correct address for all correspondence and legal documents is the same as on the summons, which was served on June 9, 1993. The correct address for all responses is 4676 Admiralty Way Suite 503, Marina Del Rey, CA 90292.

A certified mail with return receipt requested arrived June 15, 1993:

Dear Julia,

This letter is in reference to the June 11, 1993 letter. The correct address for all future communication and correspondence including your attorney's name, address, and telephone number is 4676 Admiralty Way, Suite 503, Marina Del Rey, CA 90292 not 4626 Admiralty Way. Your response is demanded immediately to the letter dated June 11, 1993. Direct all correspondence to the above address. Thank you.

Mailgram, June 15, 1993:

Dear Julia,

It's important that you get in contact with me. Not only do you have legal problems in California but you may face some criminal charges in Florida. Please contact me by leaving a message on the Florida phone number. I check the messages every day.

A certified mail with return receipt requested arrived June 16, 1993:

Dear Julia:

Please be advised that there are outstanding medical bills still due from your February 1993 dog attack. They are as follows:

1. Southeast Anesthesiology, Cole Associates: the account numbers are 0254135 - $1,092: Acct. No. 02752706 for $1,244: Acct No. 02527009800 for $77.50: Acct No. 0253477 for $1,044, for a total of $4,367.50. A check must be remitted to P.O. Box 7737, Hollywood, FL 33081. Telephone number is (305) XXX-XXXX.

2. Memorial Hospital Outpatient Care, Account No. 0979937930324 for $1,835. Mailing address for remittance: Memorial Hospital Outpatient Care, P.O. Box 229135, Hollywood, Florida 33022-9135. Telephone number is (305) XXX-XXXX

3. Hollywood Emergency Physicians, Account No. H00o366774579 for $330. It must be paid in care of First Collect Inc. P.O. Box 222660, Hollywood, FL 33022-22660.

4. Ambulance Billing, Account No. 00019101 for $236.50. It must be paid to Ambulance Billing, P.O. Box 6669, Hollywood, FL 33081. Telephone number is (305) XXX-XXXX.

The total amount of these bills is $6,759. Since you have the entire amount of the insurance proceeds, which was supposed to pay these bills, I demand you pay these within 72 hours of receipt of this letter. If not, I will be forced to seek an emergency hearing from the court ordering you to pay, and, if you continue to ignore this along with the emergency order to pay, I will ask for a writ of bodily attachment. In other words, the sheriff will come out, pick you up, bring you before the judge, and ask you why you have not paid these bills when you have the insurance money.

You have ignored everything that has been sent to you so far, and the time for ignoring is over. Please direct all communications, checks, etc., to the above address, and once again, include your attorney's name, address and telephone number. Thank you.

Branden and I drove down to meet with the lawyer in Laguna Beach, and I gave him a $5,000 retainer to begin divorce proceedings, as the ex is suing me in Florida, New York, and Los Angeles. This really was an ugly divorce, but the lawyer always seemed to have time to talk with my son and me.

It took about a year and a half until it was finalized. Never once did the ex give up, and the paper trail was horrendous. All this and a dog attack too.

The first letter from my lawyer dated June 23, 1993 was to thank me for the meeting that we had the previous day, it was a pleasure to meet unfortunately not under these circumstances and of course the retainer agreement for his services in the Family Law matter. He also let me know that if his services do not reach the retainer amount of $5,000, there will be a refund, but there's a clause to the effect that it may cost more than the retainer fee. He will write up a separate contract which will be handled on a contingency basis which he will prepare in the near future, and also the outline of a draft of an Order to Show Cause to request a restraining order.

Letter from Lawyer to the Ex June 27, 1993

The first letter to the ex let him know that I have retained a lawyer for Legal Separation and that representing himself is not a good idea, plus retaining a lawyer as well as a lay litigant is at a severe disadvantage in working with the court system. The letter also stated that at least for the present, I did not want any communication directly any longer, personally, in writing or otherwise, and all communications should be directed through the lawyer. It also stated that we (my lawyer and I) hope that he understands and cooperates with this request, that a court issued restraining order will be processed, and they are expensive and unpleasant. Go figure.

Letter from My Lawyer to the Aviation Lawyer June 27, 1993

My lawyer let the aviation lawyer know that I had retained his services for the dog attack on February 14, 1993 and that he would like the files to be transferred to him, as I am estranged from the ex who initiated the family law proceedings here in California for a legal separation to develop into an action for dissolution of the marriage. For this reason, my lawyer asked the aviation lawyer not to furnish any further information to the ex regarding the dog attack incident.

Also, he noted both Florida and California law state that any injury to a spouse is separate property to the injured party in which the spouse has no community or other legal interests, and that the client attorney privilege between the aviation lawyer and me is now revoked, and hopefully this will be in my best interest.

July 12, 1993

The first mail for my ex billing me at my address included the bills for his mortgage lenders, charge cards, South Broward Hospital District Memorial Hospital, my income tax refund for $1,200, which was jointly filed then applied for his years of back taxes that he owed and my lawyer sends me a change of address for the IRS.

July 19, 1993

My lawyer sent me the check for the $19,592.50 for the hospital for me to endorse. He returned the endorsed check from me to the aviation lawyer to sign, then forward on to the hospital to satisfy the payment. There's hope that this check will make it back to the hospital so they can receive their money. However, my lawyer tells me that Broward County was not negligent with the dog attack, as the owners built an eight-foot fence around the yard as requested by the county following the other dog attack which happened three years earlier.

If DNA had been discovered in 1993 with this dog attack, things would be different as with O.J. Simpson, which my dad helped him with his many endorsements. He used to come to the studio to have lunch with my dad, both being USC men. However, my dad always refused when O.J. eagerly, persistently and repeatedly asked him if he could sit at my dad's table with me when my dad and I were having lunch in the commissary. O.J. later asked my dad if he could take me out on a date which my father, as nice as he was, refused to allow him to do. For the longest time, I never knew why my dad made the decision that he did, but time sure does tell.

July 20, 1993

The ex's homeowner's coverage was cancelled on May 1, 1993 for nonpayment. He then paid it with a check that bounced. Because of that, the ex and I had no insurance.

July 21, 1993

The aviation lawyer wrote back to my lawyer saying that one prior earlier incident involving the dog that attacked me is not sufficient in his eyes to hold the county responsible. How many times should the same dog be able to attack someone before it is to be sufficient? I doubt the aviation lawyer ever checked this out. I mean after all he got his $15,000 or whatever deal the ex and he had.

Meanwhile, the ex retained a female lawyer and faxed to my lawyer he will not attempt to contact me directly during this thirty-day period. But the ex wrote continuously about reconciliation and what is owed to him.

July 22, 1993

My lawyer wrote to the ex that he will commence to discovery for the purpose of harassment, not the facts in his eyes. My lawyer also sends a letter to the aviation lawyer about the check endorsed for the hospital, but it's still not there yet.

July 27, 1993

My lawyer asked the ex for his homeowner's policy after the aviation lawyer and the ex would not send him the policy when asked previously. The hospital check was still not received. Send the damn check, my God.

August 3, 1993

Having received many calls from my ex, my lawyer asked his lawyer again for a substitution of attorney to no avail. My lawyer only wanted to receive communication through my ex's lawyer, and he has instructed his office not to entertain any conversations with the ex while he is out of town.

August 6, 1993

My lawyer sent the new change of address form to the IRS.

August 9, 1993

There was more mail at my address from the ex. My lawyer sent a letter to one credit company to cancel my responsibility for the charges prior to my marriage to the ex.

August 11, 1993

The ex was no longer represented by his female lawyer because she has not been compensated and other reasons she said she cannot discuss.

August 12, 1993

There was satisfaction of the lien to the hospital. My God, it's a miracle. The monies owed to the hospital for the services they provided from the dog attack are finally getting paid. Also, my lawyer sends me a copy of an article for California Lawyers who represent senior citizens, because my sister and her husband refuse to give my mother all of her possessions. My mom is now living with Branden and me by my insistence and her desire, as she told me she was afraid of both of them.

August 13, 1993

A social worker came to my apartment, claiming someone reported me as an unfit mother. I had just picked my mom up the night before from Palmdale to come live with us. The social worker took my son into his bedroom for questioning. I called my lawyer while she was in the room with my son, and when she came out, I handed the phone to her. My lawyer asked her how much does she think I weigh and, since my son is twice my size, what is she thinking?

August 16, 1993

The ex said he is going to spend some time back in Florida with his daughter, son-in-law and grandson. How I pity them, but better them than me.

August 19, 1993

The ex demanded I send him $9,642 from the insurance policy for the remaining bills.

August 24, 1993

My lawyer counsels patience in dealing with threats from the ex.

August 26, 1993

My lawyer welcomed the ex's lawyer back in writing and added, "Rather you than me."

September 1, 1993

As the ex's female lawyer denied she is willing to represent him, he has now referred all of his credit card bills to me via my lawyer. When the ex's lawyer asked my lawyer how an overall solution can be reached with all parties, my lawyer said, "The only one that comes to mind is the old and honorable tradition of the quasi-military services to which the ex deems himself spiritually allied." My lawyer did have a great sense of humor but poor judgment in my eyes, as this was a very serious situation of someone who cannot let go and stop. Also, I really didn't feel well. I was throwing up constantly from my ex's antics and in a lot of pain.

The ex's lawyer told him to stop trying to contact me, and if he does call, I'm to hang up on him. My telephone number has always been unlisted (my father insisted upon it), but the ex has my number, and I do a lot of hanging up on him for sure.

September 8, 1993

My lawyer wrote to the ex's lawyer regarding the social worker coming to my apartment and wanted to see the ex's telephone bills for that period, as he believed this was an unwarranted act of harassment and a breach of the protective orders in the Family Law Summons. My lawyer also told me I am the only person as Branden's mother to make an inquiry from the Department of Children's Services. I did. Anonymous.

September 10, 1993

The ex's lawyer was adamant that the ex did not call the social worker and that possibly there was a third party involved, as an anonymous woman called a helicopter company claiming that the ex is a wife abuser and child molester. Well, whoever called at least got that right. It wasn't me, but I have a pretty good idea who it was.

September 14, 16 and 21, 1993

Stacks of mail were sent to my apartment for the ex.

September 22, 1993

My lawyer told the ex's lawyer that after reviewing my telephone records, the call to the helicopter was not from me. No kidding, I could care a less what the ex does, who he does it with, when, where or why. Just leave me alone. He's such a POS.

September 23, 1993

Lawyers from Association Financial send a letter to the ex at my address for payment of $1,210.99 on his mortgage immediately or else his house would be sold. Bet the neighbors were happy about that. No one liked the ex in his neighborhood, no one. I'm sure they didn't believe his trumped-up fantasies and stories about himself and saw right through him. I was too late, but I did figure him out.

September 28, 1993

The ex wanted to reconcile. No, never, not a chance in hell, in fact, I was living in hell with this monster who won't quit.

October 4 and 12, 1993

More mail arrives.

October 11, 1993

My lawyer wrote back to his lawyer that there were no long distance calls from my phone bill. Go figure.

October 29, 1993

My lawyer wrote to my ex that for someone who keeps talking about reconciliation, he certainly has a strange way of doing it. He told him he is in receipt of a copy of a Summons and Petition for Dissolution of Marriage filed in the circuit court of the 17th Judicial District of Broward County, Fla. In my lawyer's perspective, there was already a pending dissolution action in California that the ex initiated, and my lawyer believed this to be in bad faith and arguably malicious.

My lawyers said if necessary he will respond and seek sanctions in Florida and California courts for his contumacious conduct as well as an order for the ex to pay for costs and attorney fees in both actions. He also told the ex that his failure to work remuneratively to support himself or me was an attempt to live off the proceeds of my unfortunate tragedy, and that there were enough proceeds from his Florida property, if he still owns it, to allow me to recover my attorney costs that he is causing as well as my emotional damages and other injuries his conduct is causing. If my lawyer did not hear from the ex that he withdraws the petition in Florida, he would proceed accordingly.

November 10, 1993

The ex wrote to my lawyer that he still wants to reconcile. Nope, never.

November 11, 1993

The hospital bill has finally been paid. Not bad; it only took eight months. My God, we're trail blazers, just call us pioneers, we know how to get the job done. My lawyer replied to yet another letter from the ex, who again wanted to reconcile. He told the ex that he's tired of him saying that he has half interest to the settlement money and how the proceeds were used to pay medical bills, etc., and that he has already received a part of those proceeds. My lawyer also wrote a letter to the ex's lawyer that strongly told her that she was not to be involved in any way in these efforts.

November 15, 1993

I had another attorney in Florida representing me in a Florida action unbeknownst to both myself and my lawyer for another restraining order injunction relief and affirmative relief one day before the hearing is to take place. The new Florida lawyer prayed that the court will issue me a restraining order against the ex, as the ex will not cease in filing actions from Florida to California and vice versa. The ex sent my California lawyer faxes for the restraining order and rescinded the open extension, and the Florida lawyer wrote a letter to me telling me that he will represent me if I will pay him on or before November 16, 1993 the amount of $2,000. I have no idea who the hell this guy is. Let me thank him in advance for allowing me to pay him. In the end, I never even met him.

November 17, 1993

The ex decides to set some people for depo, the aviation lawyer being one of them. Then the ex writes in a letter that I was raving to the aviation lawyer on the one and only time I spoke with him, you bet I was and I was furious with both of them. Scam artists.

November 18, 1993

My lawyer tells me the ex is going to take my deposition and my lawyer wants a description of the ex. My lawyer also writes to the ex at all of his many addresses and tells him he must furnish him with a change of address letter or pick a place to live.

December 1, 1993

The Florida lawyer sends me another bill for $48.50. Why, I don't know.

CHAPTER 16 – MORE SHENANIGANS BEFORE CLOSURE

It only takes one bad decision to send your life reeling into the toilet. My life by the start of 1994 was one living hell of a nightmare. My son, my fragile mom and I can't enjoy one day of peace and healing, as we have endured the ex's antics and thought that this is taking way too long for a ten-month marriage to dissolve. Oh, I forgot, a dog attack too.

January 3, 1994

The ex wrote to the Florida lawyer that even though I don't want to speak with him, he's sure we both love each other. Yuck, I think I just threw up a little bit again. He changes his mind from moment to moment, which he says is due to male menopause, and he's gone back to discovery in Florida and California in case one is dismissed. He wrote that no one is paying attention to him and that he wanted what was legally his even to the point of criminal prosecution against me.

The ex added that he's living in Big Bear, Calif., his girlfriend is out of town, and he loves me. What a freak. The Florida lawyer writes to my lawyer and says he's not taking any of the ex's calls, as he doesn't want to waste his time.

January 4, 1994

My lawyer sent me more correspondence from the ex.

January 19, 1994

My lawyer wrote to the ex at the Marina Del Rey and Florida addresses in care of his sister and told him to pick one address, plus insisted that the ex respond to the Family Law Form Interrogatories, Request for Admissions and a set of Specially Prepared Interrogatories that were served upon him June 27, 1993 with no response received. My lawyer also told me that he is going to try to recover the monies I gave the ex and get restraining orders on him. I think we're finally on a roll now.

January 29, 1994

My lawyer wrote to the ex that he is in receipt by telecopy of the ex's letter to my lawyer saying that as much as he tries, he cannot ignore all of his communications. Again my lawyer asked the ex for his official address that the ex either failed to receive or refused to acknowledge, a real address where he can receive this action for emergency relief hearings. My lawyer told the ex that courts frown upon exercises that give notice designed not to be received, that he needed to correct himself, and that his statement to the Florida courts look like deliberate misstatements made for the purpose of accomplishing litigate advantage.

My lawyer also told the ex that he does not get to pick and choose when, where and what time but to do as he is told, that he will seek sanctions and that the ex's refusal to answer questions under oath would be underlying the facts. He added that I will refuse to speak with my ex and that the ex has failed with the agreement he made to both me and my lawyer to stop harassing me.

Also, my lawyer told the ex he could anticipate restraining orders on him and that since my ex was remuneratively employed by his own admission, he would ask the court to pay support to me while the dissolution of marriage was pending during my state of disability. He was sure California law would concur.

My lawyer also said with respect to pending medical bills, the $10,000 given to the ex by me should be paid by him, that no other outstanding bills should go into collection efforts against me, that I should have half the interest from the house, and that those monies should be used to pay the remainder of the medical bills.

Additionally, my lawyer warns the ex that he is being observed and that any contact from his conduct is threatening and will have severe consequences. He lets the ex know that the only things to discuss are how much he is willing to pay in support and medical bills and how far away from me he will be ordered to remain from me, as any meeting with the ex will only be stressful. He informs him that appropriate protective orders will be in place for me and to stop taking advantage of the rules he is flouting for improper use.

The last thing my lawyer wrote is that when the courts read all my ex's letters with no address on many of them, the conclusion will be the same. He told my ex that he hoped he has paid enough attention to him now, and that many motions and series of notices and other moving papers are on the way to him.

Way to go for my lawyer! It doesn't work, but it's a good letter nonetheless. As you can see, the ex was desperate for attention, and this is a game that my lawyer no longer wished to entertain. Here is the letter he wrote back to my lawyer.

> Dear Julia's lawyer,
>
> This letter is in further reference to your letter of Jan. 29, 1994. With reference to the insurance question, if you look at the check made out by the insurance company, you will see that it is made out to both Julia and me and the aviation lawyer. As I have said all along, I was a claimant. This will be affirmed by the aviation lawyer and the insurance adjuster for the company in deposition. Also, let me bring to your attention the release which Julia and I both had to sign.
>
> As for the $10,000, if you look closely at the check, you will see it was made out to both Julia and me. The check was cashed at the Southeast Bank where Julia took $3,000 and put it into her pocket, and the cashier's check was made out for $7,000 to both Julia and me. This was deposited in our joint account at Citibank. This money was to pay for bills and household expenses, since I had to take six weeks off to care for Branden and Julia. This was all agreed on before leaving the aviation lawyers office on March 23, 1993, the day the funds were disbursed and will be affirmed by the aviation lawyer and two of his staff members in deposition.
>
> As for the money that was left after attorney fees, doctor fees, hospital bills and the $10,000 deduction, the total amount came to $49,000, of which Julia agreed I had an interest. Once again this was witnessed by the aviation lawyer and his staff. Julia had said that if I were to give up her control of my share of the remaining

insurance money ($49,000), she would take care of the other bills that might come up. Before leaving, the aviation lawyer cautioned Julia that there may be more medical bills coming and to be cautious on spending the money.

Since Julia greed to take care of the bills, I agreed to let Julia have control of the remaining $49,000. So the aviation lawyer made the check out to her alone. Once again, witness corroboration and document verification on this is irrefutable!

The $4,357 medical bill from the anesthesiologist did not surface until mid-April, after they had billed Prudential and the claim had been denied because we had reached policy limits. The same is true with regard to the $330 in emergency physician bills and the ambulance bill of $236. They had billed Prudential after we had settled and were unaware of these bills until mid-April. When I asked Julia to pay them, she said she would. They have yet to be paid.

As for the MRI bill, that did not surface until May. By then, Julia had left for California and taken every penny with her! The bill for her therapy from Memorial Home Health came in June and totaled $3,398.

It was pretty clear that Julia had lied to both the aviation lawyer and me. She had no intention of paying these medical bills or relinquishing my share of the $49,000, which she had been given in fiduciary trust. As it turns out, she took all of the money and put it in a trust account, under her son Branden's name, in order to keep it from me until she could leave for California. The whole time, I was constantly reassured that "everything was under control." By doing this, she opened herself up for possible criminal prosecution under Florida law.

According to the Florida attorney general's office and the Broward County state attorney's office, I have a well-documented "paper trail" on this criminal act! I'd like to bring to your attention the fact that I saved Julia and myself $18,000 in legal fees. The aviation lawyer agreed to take the case for 15 percent of any amount collected up to the time of filing suit as long as I would do the legwork. Julia and I both agreed to this.

So, if you think I just sat back and fucked off and waited for the money to come rolling in, you're way off base! I worked hard to get the money for Julia. She has a funny way of thanking me, don't you agree?

As for the house in Hollywood, Fla., Julia is a joint owner as well as a signatory on the mortgage. Oh, and she has not contributed one dime.

Now, I would suggest that you start coming up with ideas on how your client Julia is going to reimburse me for mortgage and house payments. I'm waiting patiently for these monies to appear. And I have the utmost faith in you that they will in the very near future.

Julia's car was purchased after we were married from the joint funds, so I'm sure the courts will consider it community property. I do have an interest in it.

As for harassment, I think you should know that Julia has gone through most of her life making herself out to be the poor victim. She used people to get her way, and no one ever questioned her. I, on the other hand, know exactly what she's all about. That's why she's so adamant about not seeing me and making my life hell at the moment! I am not the harassing party in this situation, and Julia is not the "poor" victim, she's just afraid to face what she's done and face the truth of this whole matter. For the first time in her life, Julia is made to face what her actions have done to someone else.

Yes, Lawyer, I could probably forgive her for everything she's done. But is she going to keep making up excuses? Is she going to keep making up stories in hopes that everything that happened to her will go away? I don't know. If it wasn't for that damn dog attack, we would still be together, I have no doubt. Julia and I had a pretty good marriage. I miss her and I love her, even after all of the shit she's put me through.

In closing, if Julia wants spousal support she's going to have to go back being a spouse.

P.S. Don't get excited about the California postmark. As I stated in a February 2, 1994 letter, I came out for a purpose. I don't intend to stay.

P.P.S. I'm sending a Fed Ex package for Julia. It is something for her for Valentine's Day. It may be her dream come true. You can review it and pass it on to her. Instructions will be enclosed. Thanks.

Well, what a wonderful caring letter! I was told to put the money in $10,000 increments before we left and that's what I did. Nothing was in my son's name, and no, I'm not a victim. I was a working actress for many years, and this tool came out of nowhere, my mistake, and then the dog attack. What a pig,

Again, I have often wondered why when I was in the hospital for two weeks no one ever came by to speak with me. Not a social worker, lawyer or even a representative from the hospital came to give me some advice. The ex kept everyone away from me, and no one ever asked him to do anything to remedy this horrible situation. Certainly not me.

If the aviation lawyer and the ex were such good friends, and his employer, why did he want $15,000? I don't think under the circumstances anyone would have to work hard with the tragic events, while I was in the hospital or want any money at all. In fact, the aviation lawyer asked me for another $8,000 of which the ex owed him for long distance phone bills in his office prior to us knowing each other. I told the aviation lawyer that I would not be paying the ex's bills.

As far as his comments about being a victim my whole life, I can assure you, I've worked my whole life since I was six. And outside of a crazy actress and my sister and brother in-law, the people in Hollywood will tell you quite a different story.

I am a victim to a dog attack, and by my own doing, I married a really bad person, a liar and a manipulator who's very dangerous. Yes, I'm guilty of that, and as a friend of mine told me, "Bad people should be exposed." Thank God I didn't give the aviation lawyer or the ex any more money, at least for now.

February 2, 1994

OK, now here's where things really get funny. Of course none of this is funny, but when you lived through all of this and read through all of these documents, one must keep their sense of humor with such a dangerous person.

My lawyer wrote in response to the ex's letter that Charles Dickens wrote *A Tale of Two Cities*. The ex now is a big movie man working with producers and directors and that I am being considered for the lead role to play opposite a very well-known actor. Oh please.

For a guy who's never been to Hollywood, he sure seems to know a lot of stars. I guess his bullshit gets him in somehow or maybe someone is helping him. It could be that actress who screwed everyone in Hollywood, such a treacherous female. Here's the letter from my ex to my lawyer.

I'm in receipt of your Jan. 28, 1994 letter. I suggest that you have your eyes checked when you read. I have really had it. You have done more to screw up Julia and my marriage that we could have done in a lifetime. What started out as a simple separation and possibly a missed communication between Julia and I has now gone to a level that makes the movie *War of the Roses* look tame, all because you have refused to sit down and discuss things, and you have encouraged Julia to do the same.

It has been more through your threatening letters and condescending and provoking manner that you have brought us to this point. You have been able to take us further apart through your manipulation actions/ After working ten years with the aviation lawyer and part of this time with the Florida Bar and (another man), an attorney with the Florida Bar, I've seen attorneys violate the Canon of Ethics, but you definitely take the cake.

However, you've not only done damage to me, but also your client. In my last letter, I advised you that I need to speak with Julia about her career. I have had some limited involvement in pre-production and production of an upcoming movie about the French Revolution based on a novel by Victor Hugo (the man who wrote *A Tale of Two Cities*), which will be partially filmed in France and the United States.

The producer and director are looking to cast (father and son actors) in the movie. They were looking for a female lead to co-star opposite (the son). Because of my friendship with the producer and director, through my aviation contacts and using the *Hard Copy* tape of Julia's accident as a current video, I was able to get them to consider Julia for the part. They agreed that she would fit the part rather well. However, because of her past conduct in Hollywood, they were hesitant to use her. I assured them I would see that Julia acted as a true professional.

As a personal favor, they gave me a copy of the script and advised me to bring her in for a reading and discuss a contract by February 1, 1994. To say the contract was lucrative would be an understatement. Since Julia had been advised by you not to talk with me, and you seem to never read the letters or pass on vital information to her, I feel because of this communication problem, you may have cost her a major shot at getting her career back together.

But of course, in this phase of her life, since it has nothing to do with the pending litigation, I can see where you would not do anything in her best interest. And I really feel you have not had her best interest in mind, except how much money you can get from Julia or me and how you can show off trying to intimidate people. Well, intimidation does not work with me. I should have known that as active as you've been in the Los Angeles court system as a defendant in a number of civil cases, where suit has been brought against you personally, and the fact you've moved your office four times in ten years, in my opinion, you are not what I'd call an ideal attorney.

As for your letter of Jan. 28, 1994, let me bring a few points to your attention, which you overlooked. Let's first start with (Florida Lawyer) Notice of Unavailability. The date of unavailability on that was from Feb. 28, 1994 to March 8, 1994. My hearing on (Florida Lawyer) Motion to Dismiss, after taking into consideration (Florida lawyer) Notice of Unavailability, I scheduled a Motion for Feb. 8, 1994. Once again you failed to read correspondence or the Motion and the Notice.

As for your Interrogatories, I have no problem answering them (read my response letter of Nov. 18, 1993, which you received by fax on 11:11 a.m. on Nov. 29, 1993). I have simply been waiting for the jurisdictional question to be resolved. Read my letter to you dated Jan. 28, 1994. As for my phone number, once again, you simply don't read the mail or faxes. You have had it since Nov. 29, 1993.

As for harassment, I have not been near or around Julia since the last time we saw each other on Aug. 10, 1993. For that matter, I have not even been around Marina Del Rey since then. As for phone calls, I don't think four phone calls in four months to find out what Julia's going to do about the thousands of dollars in unpaid bills she left behind in Florida is harassment. I would have rather spoke with her than have to file a waterfall of motions in order to get the same answer. That is the only reason I'd call her, and because both she and you have either ignored the issues or continually to refuse to address the issue that Julia has chosen to run from.

As for the fact that you have stated in your Feb. 28, 1994 letter that you have me under observation, and after a long conversation and meeting with the FBI this morning, it is believed you are conspiring either knowingly or unknowingly with Julia and other unnamed persons to stalking me. This conclusion is partially based on a phone conversation that Julia had with a former friend (note: that actress again!) on Dec. 2, 1993 wherein Julia had advised (that actress again) that Julia and her boyfriend wanted to kill me.

It is also based on the fact there were phone calls that were made to my sister and Julia's brother-in-law and sister from a man saying he was from Arizona wanting to know my whereabouts. Since I know no one in Arizona, these calls were brought to the attention of law enforcement and apparently have been traced back to Julia's phone number. The voice that was identified on the call and the boyfriend of Julia have been identified as one and the same. I have a meeting next week with California law enforcement officers with reference to this stalking issue and your letter.

As for the possibility of your request for spousal support, let's look at the facts. We were married for eleven months and have been separated for nine months. Julia's gross income for the three years prior to our marriage was $5,000 per year. She did not work at all during our marriage, and as I understand it, Julia's been holding down several jobs with no problem.

It will be interesting to see if Julia all of a sudden becomes unemployed during the time you've scheduled the hearing for spousal support and if all of a sudden Julia's arm begins to bother her. I can just see it now: Julia has re-injured her arm as a result of the earthquake. Again, it will be quite a coincidence, since I understand from a mutual friend that she not only receives money from her mother who is living with her, but also a boyfriend who is living with them who is supporting her.

There are a number of other issues in your Feb. 28, 1994 letter which we will address as they come up. Moreover, as each hearing is set and heard, I fully intend to bring your latest letter to the court's attention.

I can't believe I've finally made contact with a real prophet, someone who can foresee the future and prophesied what decision the courts are going to make. I truly believe once word gets through the court system, your practice and your riches will abound.

Regarding what my ex stated in this letter, Hollywood is a business. I find it extremely hard to believe that an actor of such consummate acclaim would lend an ear to a layperson who's not even in the industry. This business will eat you up and spit you out any time it deems appropriate. Hollywood can be forgiving or not. This town does not have an open door policy. One reason there are guards at every single entrance at every single studio is just for con artists like the ex. If it were that easy to get onto the lots or into the business, everyone would be a star, director, producer or writer. It just doesn't happen like that. Not even with such great aviation contacts.

February 4, 1994

The Florida lawyer sent me a letter that a notice of hearing was set by the ex in Florida to make every effort to keep the Florida case open. He said he needs $588.50 plus an additional $1,000, and that the notice of hearing is in Judge XYZ court and not Judge ABC at 8:30 am February 4, 1994. Who is this guy?

A letter from the ex to my lawyer on February 11, 1994:

Dear Professor .....,

Last night I spoke with XXX, the screenwriter who wrote the script which I hope you have by now. He advised me the script is based on the novel *93* by Victor Hugo. Thank you for correcting my illiterate mind on French Revolution writers and novels. It's nice to know my wife can afford to help me continue with my education, especially at the rate of $275 per hour. I knew she cared!

Now to a more serious subject. It looks like I'll be stuck here in the L.A. area through Monday. After your letter of Jan. 29, 1994, I've had time to calm down a little. I would like to make a very serious proposal. Please believe me, I think I finally got my heart and mind working together.

Let me start off by saying I love Julia more than any woman I can remember (and I think I've got a pretty good memory). A while back, Julia and I agreed on one point, we loved each other and probably would till the day we died, whether we stayed together or not. I'd like to believe that still holds true.

Over the last few months, we've gone the gamut of one upmanship in order to protect the interest of each party. You've even admitted your growing tired of it, and I think I'm beginning to finally feel the effects also. Not to mention the monetary cost are going way out of sight. I know Julia's got to be hurting for money if after nine months of separation she's all of a sudden starting to push the spousal support issue.

So my proposal is as follows. We can call a halt to the current litigation and attempt to try to rebuild the marriage. I will voluntarily dismiss the Florida action and leave open the California action. If after a certain period of time, once we gotten back together, we still cannot resolve our problems, then we walk away, both seeking nothing from the other. I will agree to limited spousal support if Julia agrees to give the marriage one more chance. And to dissolve the marriage if needed under California law. I also propose that everything that is agreed to is put in writing to prevent future misunderstandings.

I hope when you pass this proposal on to Julia, you give her all the good and bad points, and I hope she will listen.

A while back, we spoke at length when I saw you as less of an adversary and more of a wise man. You spoke of what you went through when you and your wife separated, and how you had to take a long look at yourself and make some changes. Perhaps my time has come for the long look and changes, as I'm sure Julia has had time to think also.

As we get closer to the anniversary of the dog attack (Valentine's Day), I can't help but think of what Julia's gone through in the past year. Perhaps I'll never really know because I never spent a day in her shoes. But my heart goes out to her. What she has suffered, no one should have to suffer. Unless you were there to see what happened, you'll never really know. It was something I would not wish on my worst enemy.

In closing, I hope Julia listens to this proposal and thinks it out before she says "No." Because in the end, there are no winners, even if you get what you want, and wounds sometimes never heal.

Well, he's right about one thing. Some wounds never do heal. As far as another chance, let me tell you this: if it looks like a duck, walks like a duck and quakes like a duck, it's a duck. How the hell can you love someone that you hardly know or that's like him? I've had plenty of time to think, my answer isn't no, it's "Fuck no!" I may have been slow and trusting, but I'm not stupid. This monster should have thought about one thing even before the dog attack, how dare he put hands on my son ever, not to mention me too. May God help him, because he's a very sick being and should be locked up for his heinous actions with a beautiful child and mother and to save other women and children, even his own.

February 24, 1994

The Florida lawyer sent me the Notice of Hearing for March 17, 1994 at 8:45 a.m. with the judge in Broward County by the ex and the motions from the Florida lawyer to dismiss.

March 3, 1994

My lawyer wrote to the ex, giving him one last chance to respond to discovery, and warned the ex that since he is the one filing motions everywhere, he will seek sanctions for what is clearly on the ex's behalf a refusal to respond to discovery.

A handwritten letter from my ex to my lawyer on March 4, 1994:

I'm sure by now you have received my handwritten Motion to Dismiss, which has been scheduled for March 22, 1994 at 8:30 am Dept. J. Please be advised in the next few days you will be receiving a much neater and more detailed Amended Motion to Dismiss (typewritten), along with several other Motion and Pleadings. Sorry for the sloppy motion, it's being corrected.

I'm leaving California to go overseas for a few days, then returning home to Florida. I need to know by March 15, 1994, if Julia is interested in the part in the movie *1793* and if you passed on the script which I asked you to pass on to her. I must have an answer in writing.

A letter from my lawyer to the ex on March 11, 1994:

I am in receipt of your purported "Amended Notice of Motion, etc." Don't you ever learn?

In my letter to you on March 7, 1994. I informed you of two things: First, that under the California Code of Civil Procedure, the notice that you attempted to give by mail on March 2, 1994 for a hearing on March 2, 1994 was already inadequate (that's lawyer talk for "too short"); serving a purported "amended notice" on March 7, 1994 obviously cannot make it any more adequate. I also told you that I have a conflict with a previously calendared trial; that conflict still exists.

While I want to be cautious about giving legal advice to one so obviously learned in the law, I believe that persevering in a course that will require me to make an appearance at an inadequately noticed motion, and incur not only the basic expense, but the additional expense (and/or inconvenience to the Court and counsel in the other matter) and which will be denied for that reason, particularly after the defect has been pointed out to you, is the kind of "frivolous" conduct that is made sanctionable by Code of Civil Procedure 128.5, even on the part of a lay litigant. This is not a threat, but the warning I am required under the Code to give as a condition precedent to a request for sanctions.

Finally, it is considered uncool to threaten appeals.

March 17, 1994

My lawyer was really pissed off and started a moving paper trail from hell. He will not cooperate with the ex's antics anymore, or his aviation lawyer either, and prays to the court that I can have the protective orders and my divorce.

My lawyer is very schooled in the law and sends lots of papers to the ex. Here's his letter to the ex's friend, the aviation lawyer, on April 12, 1994.

On behalf of Julia Benjamin, whom I represent in the above captioned action, you are hereby instructed that all communications between you and Ms. Benjamin, on any matter whatsoever, and whether or not Mr. Ex was a party or privy to such communications, including all communications with the undersigned, Ms. Benjamin attorney (including this and any accompanying letter, as well as our prior correspondence and oral communication), and all oral and written communications and correspondence between you and any other person, and all research, writings, notes, memoranda and other products of your efforts as attorney, are deemed to be within the attorney-client privilege and/or the attorney work-product privilege, respectively. All documents and/or information in your possession, custody, control and/or knowledge about Ms. Benjamin, including but not limited to her personal and other financial affairs, deriving from such communications, are deemed by Ms. Benjamin to be within the privilege(s).

Accordingly, you are hereby expressly instructed by Ms. Benjamin, as the holder of the privilege(s), that you are not to disclose, discuss or reveal, the whole or any party thereof to any person, expressly including but not necessarily limited to the ex, and that the foregoing prohibition expressly extends to any deposition or other testimony, document production or other discovery sought from you by the ex in the above-captioned case and/or in any other action or proceeding, whether under California or Florida Jurisdiction.

You are further instructed by Ms. Benjamin to report the undersigned any attempt by the ex to penetrate aforementioned privileges. Any argument that The Ex may care to raise that, for whatever reason, the attorney-client or attorney work product privileges do not exist or are not applicable, will first have to be addressed to the California Court, and, until that Court has made a definitive ruling herein, you are bound by the forgoing instruction.

If there are any questions or problems, please do not hesitate to call.

Well we're getting there. My lawyer finally sees the impact of the ex's stalking, harassment, threats, and his inability to stop.

A letter from my lawyer to the ex April 13, 1994:

I am in receipt by telecopy of your letter April 6, 1994. In response, you are hereby notified, on behalf of Ms. Benjamin, that she will, and hereby does, object to any attempt on your part to cause the taking of a physical or physiological examination in the above captioned matter, on the grounds that include, but are not necessarily limited to, irrelevance to the subject matter of the action and the lack of a reasonable possibility of leading to discovery of admissible evidence, violation of rights of privacy under the laws and constitution of the State of California and the United States, and on the further ground that such examination or examinations would be burdensome and oppressive.

Accordingly, you may do whatever it is you attempted to say you would do if I should "choose not to cooperate." You may deem this letter as a choice not to cooperate.

I do admonish you, however, that any attempt on your part to compel the taking of such examination will be deemed not only frivolous, but as an intentional attempt on your part to inflict emotional distress upon and to harass Ms. Benjamin, and will not only be vigorously opposed, but will be met with a request for sanctions.

A final matter: The rules of the court, even in family matters, require appropriate courtesies to be maintained between parties and attorneys. In the future, please refrain from the use of Ms. Benjamin's first name and from referring to her by her first name in correspondence or moving papers; she and I find it overly familiar under the circumstances of the case. In connection with the foregoing, please be advised that Ms. Benjamin, as is her right, has exercised her election to use her former name, Benjamin, exclusively; she is no longer known as and will not respond to either "……" or "Benjamin-."

Boy I'll tell you, my dad must be rolling in his grave at this point, God rest his soul. While in California, the ex now contacts my mom's friend. The ex involves himself with everybody he can from my day timer, whether he has ever met them or not.

Meanwhile, my mom's friend really wasn't a friend to her at all, and she was a busybody from the word go. Her friend just wouldn't leave my sister alone. She called her and told her that my mom was going to take a world cruise and that she has a little money from the death of my dad. Consequently, that would be the reason that my sister and brother-in-law would sell her house in Calabasas and have her move in with them. I warned my mom not to do that ,but she did anyway, and while Branden and I were living in New York, my mom's girlfriend called to tell me that my sister and brother-in-law would not let her have any visitors or contact with anyone she knew. I told my mom's friend that I knew that was going to happen and asked why she couldn't mind her own business.

My mom's friend and husband were accountants and frequently invested. However, my mom always got the short end of the stick with their investment advice and never really made any money from it. They didn't mind taking her money.

Unfortunately, my parents were so kind and trusting but really didn't have good judgment in their later years with the friends that used them. That was because my dad was a casting director and hired people that he thought were his friends. Another couple that were their friends used to claim that weren't just friends because my father was a casting director over fifty years, even though the husband was an actor. But I tell you when my dad passed, my mom was dropped from many of their so-called friends, and she was so lonely and so sad after losing my dad that it broke my heart.

So here's a letter to my mom's girlfriend the accountant from my ex, and as usual, he refers to me to my limited lack of education. If my parents taught me anything about being a good person, the one important thing was how to treat people; you can't make someone like or love you, period. The ex just can't accept rejection, as you will see the antics of his behavior once again.

April 12, 1994

I've just arrived back in California for a few days, and I wanted to write you a letter to say thank you for taking the time to speak with me last month. I had forgotten that it was tax time, so you'll have to forgive my untimely call.

The call, as I explained, was twofold. First of course, (my sister and brother in-law's) concern for (my mom). Whether or not their concern was real, only time will tell. As for the second reason, it looks like I may have to subpoena your copies of Julia's tax records. I am however hoping that Julia and her attorney will cooperate in the normal discovery process and a subpoena for your records will not be necessary.

It is truly sad that our marriage has come to this point. I don't think Julia and I have ever stop loving each other. However we are both hardheads. If you ask each of us whether we love each other on any given day, you might find our response different from the day before.

I think the fact comes down to the point that Julia does things and then doesn't realize the consequences of her action till it is too late, then runs away, fearing that someone's mad at her and hoping that everything will go away. Whereas in our case, if she ever talks with me, she'll find I'm not mad, and in fact I think I probably learned to understand her better that anyone else ever has.

Another sad consequence of this whole mess is Julia believes that when a motion on a pleading is filed in our divorce case, that it's a personal attack on her, when in reality it's just the normal course of litigation. I think that since Julia's education is so limited, her attorney has made her believe that this is my way of being vindictive. Nothing could be further from the truth.

However, as I look back on ten years with a Florida law firm, I come to realize that litigation in any form is a vindictive process, even though it's not meant to be that way. Although when you're dealing with a limited education like Julia has and emotions are running high, especially in a divorce case, everything is considered to be vindictive. And the final conclusion is there are no winners in a divorce.

Lord knows I've tried to talk to Julia and tried to reason and reconciled with her. I know financially and emotionally she'd find herself a lot better off. I'm sure she'll find it a lot easier to deal with

Branden and her mother. But as the saying goes, she can't see the forest for the trees. Reconciliation is cheaper that divorce.

I know if it wasn't for the dog attack, we'd still be together. I do know one thing for sure after speaking to a number of people who have known Julia for a long time. Every one of them has said the same thing, that when they talked to Julia before the dog attack, it seemed that she finally found the happiness she'd been looking for, for so long. And that's the saddest part of this whole thing, the brief happiness that she had waited so long for. She may not be able to recover, even though she could if she'd just sit down and think a little.

Anyway, in closing, it was a pleasure talking with you, and thank you once again for taking the time to speak with me. Please excuse this sloppy letter, but I'm beginning to feel like a coast to coast yo-yo.

Well, now this piece of shit wanted to see my taxes after a ten-month marriage and a dog attack. Again he just can't stop, and he loves to put me down constantly, but when you have a short man's complex and are impotent—which I found out on the evening of our marriage—I guess you have a hard time living in your own skin. Maybe that's why this whole thing happened.

One thing for sure, I can't stand this asshole. He's a bully, he can't or won't keep his hands off me or my son, and he's unable to control himself on any level, signs to surely look out for with an obsessive person with mental disorders. All I want is a divorce and for him to leave me, my mom and son alone.

But he just isn't able to, or can't or doesn't have the ability to. I'd say it's sad, but let's face it—this is very scary. Thank God I survived. I know so many others in my shoes wouldn't have been able to get away.

Oh, and trust me, my sister and brother-in-law had no concern for my mother. They just wanted her monthly check which, when I went through the bills after I moved my mom in with us, was for men's boxers, horse feed, children's clothes and nothing for my mom. At least I did the very best I could for her in the end, and every penny of her money was spent on her for her cigarettes or medicine—anything she wanted, anything.

Meanwhile, the ex just doesn't get it. It's over—it was a long time ago. I really distain and hate him, and the only way I would ever have seen or had a conversation with him is if he was on life support, so you figure out the outcome. What a vindictive monster. No love inside him for anyone or anything. In the end, the dog attack was better. At least they put the dog down.

One other thing: I'm so tired of being referred to having "limited education." Hollywood sure didn't seem to think so. Four hours of school and four hours of work, for a working child on the set. That's the law, and I was a straight A student.

Through my many years of working in Hollywood, you see so many people that will always be on the outside looking in and never on the inside looking out. I will always remember that my dad told me that many times, he had seen an actress where the boyfriend or husband have screwed up more careers in Hollywood by interfering with their career in hopes to be a part of the fame and recognition of Hollywood. I truly believe this is the case here. Oh, and the money. The ex never stops talking about the money, but make your own decision with these documents, of which I hold all the hard copies written in his hand and letterheads from the lawyers. OK, back to the movie.

April 18, 1994

My lawyer wrote back to the ex that he objects him taking my deposition and it is now apparent that a motion for protective order is necessary. This has become like the hospital check for $19,000. Think I will ever get that order? We shall see.

April 19, 1994

My lawyer enclosed the ex's responses to interrogatories propounded by him. The ex was in the process of moving and would not have a fixed address for some period of time. My lawyer also wrote to the aviation lawyer saying that he objects to him providing a copy to the deposition report. Additionally, my lawyer was surprised to learn that the deposition of the aviation lawyer and his secretary was scheduled with no notice. My lawyer was even more surprised that no subpoena has been issued, and he told the aviation lawyer that the Florida depositions are an attempt to harass and oppress me.

April 22, 1994

The trial has been set for June 8, 1994. My lawyer now refers to the ex as "what's his name," and we will prepare for this in the near future. Good name for him. I can think of several others.

April 26, 1994

My lawyer sent copies of all correspondence and pleadings to a Hollywood, Florida address, and told the ex again to choose one address. The ex sent Notice of Continuance of the taking of my deposition from April 27 at 10 a.m. to May 17 at 1:30 p.m. at a Wilshire office in Los Angeles. The ex requested all of my W-2 and 1099 forms from Jan. 1, 1989 to present and all documents from the Screen Actors Guild too.

A letter to my lawyer from the ex April 29, 1994:

This is a letter to inform you that the hearing that was held on April 29, 1994 before the Commissioner (name withheld) in Department J of the Los Angeles Superior Court, West District has granted my application to continue trial date until July 11, 1994 with a discovery cut-off date of June 24, 1994.

Also, please be advised that the commissioner has ordered that you stipulate to the taking of depositions out of state. Let me inform you that during the hearing proceedings, your associate who appeared on your behalf acted in the most unprofessional manner by not introducing herself and advising that she was substitute counsel for hearing. During the hearing, your associate advised the court of an irrelevant issue, the allegation that there has been issued a restraining order against me and numerous police reports because I was stalking Julia. Before the hearing was held, I reviewed the court file as the docketing book, and I could see no restraining order.

Secondly, I have made an overt effort to stay as clear away of Julia, including the City of Marina Del Rey. As for the police reports, I am having someone check in the County of Los Angeles and in the city of Marina Del Rey for any that have been made. I can account for 100 percent of my time over the last 12 months. And I can assure you that if I continue to hear these malicious and unfounded allegations of false police reports and alleged unfounded motions which I have not been advised of, I will not only take civil action—you can expect criminal prosecution. It seems as though Julia is being vindictive and malicious because of her inability to handle rejection.

I will endeavor to work with you in anyway in order to make the stipulations to take the depositions of my witnesses in Florida as easy as possible. However, I will seek sanctions for whatever other remedies the California code of Civil Procedure provides. Please govern yourself accordingly.

While the ex sent his paper trail back and forth for months, you can clearly see that he used all the terminology that my lawyer used to address his antics. My lawyer sent his partner to the hearing that was initiated by the ex and gave her time to review all the ex's documents and especially his bizarre behavior, so she did not have any interest in speaking with the ex or introducing herself. Inside the courthouse, the ex followed her into the woman's bathroom and put himself right up in her face, then he cornered her by one of the stalls and would not let her leave until he finished his threats to her.

This is how the ex behaves and handles any situation where he is rejected and fails to receive enough attention. My lawyer was hired to handle all this for me, so he did not need my consent of what to write or how to go forward with the proceedings with a divorce. However, the ex thinks he is above the law even to the point of being inside the courthouse and following a lawyer into the woman's bathroom so he can do whatever he wants to anyone he wants. Sick!

May 1, 1994

My lawyer wrote to his partner that laughter is the best medicine and misery loves company, referring to the ex. He wrote to the ex that the Family Law form Interrogatories that were sent to him omitted the blank Schedule of Assets and Debts and blank income and Expense Declaration forms. This is how the ex would handle things to his advantage—always being incomplete so he can buy more time to harass me and squander more of the money that I'm running out of quickly thanks to him. But I think that was the whole point.

My lawyer told the ex that my financial resources are being drained by the necessity of defending myself constantly against his antics, and that if he would just go away and waive all his claims, my lawyer would waive my claims against him. At this point we can all see the ex is a dangerous person, vindictive, filled with hate and living in a delusional state of mind. Of course, he can't control himself. My lawyer told him that I have asked my lawyer to communicate to the ex that rejection is exactly what I want more than anything else.

Another letter the same date stated that the court on the ex's behalf has sent his application and continued the trial to July 11 and that the Florida lawyer sent me a bill for $1,085.75. The same date, my lawyer objected to the ex taking my deposition again, as my lawyer believes the intended purpose is for harassing and oppressing me. Once again, who is this guy, the Florida lawyer? More money for what? I sure as hell don't see any results anywhere.

May 5, 1994

My lawyer wrote to the Florida lawyer that he is getting a conformed copy of the California court's order, and if the ex refuses to dismiss that, he will make the necessary costs and appearances.

May 6, 1994

My lawyer wrote to the ex that he has received an Order to Show Cause in the Florida courts to appear, that the California Court has the jurisdiction and that the pending case will be dismissed. He will make an award for the attorney's fees, and he is giving the ex seven days to respond and act accordingly. Seriously, do you think this asshole knows how to act accordingly? NO, he does not.

May 11, 1994

The Florida lawyer wrote to my lawyer to tell him that he has withdrawn from the case unless he receives $1,085.75. I'm so tired of paying lawyers due to the antics of the ex running all around back and forth from Florida to California, setting motions and costing me more than $10,000, I can't get any results for a ten-month marriage and a dog attack.

May 13, 1994

My lawyer responded to a Motion and Request for default in the Circuit Court of the 17th Judicial Circuit in and for Broward County, Fla., regarding Associates Financial Services of America, being that the ex's house is in the ex's name, mine and two other people, whoever they are—I've never heard of them.

May 16, 1994

The ex sent my lawyer a notice that he will be taking the depositions of my sister and brother-in-law on May 31 at 9:30 a.m. in Littlerock, Calif., before a certified shorthand reporter, signed by the ex, and also that actress, scheduled for June 1 at 9:30 a.m. on Wilshire Boulevard before a certified shorthand reporter too. She is always in the picture, ho of Hollywood, pig of pigs. As my mother always said, "Sleep with pigs, wake up smelling like a pig." Also, these documents were executed in Whittier, Calif., yet the ex claims he does not live in California. My lawyer sends me copies of the documents.

May 18, 1994

Today is my deposition with the ex, which he set up, and my lawyer came by to pick me up. I remembered the idea of ever seeing this monster again made me sick, literally sick, and so my lawyer, having endured all of his antics, asked me if I wanted to really piss off the ex. Of course, I said yes.

So my lawyer told me to make the ex think that we (my lawyer and I) are having an affair. I did, and was he ever furious. I never looked at him once during the deposition, where came up with yet more harassment and claimed there was witness tampering by my lawyer. Of course, only a fool represents himself.

By the time the deposition was over, my lawyer and I walked out to his car. I asked him how I did. We laughed so hard on the way to the car, and my lawyer told me even he thought we were having an affair (FYI, my lawyer was married).

And so the ex left a message at my lawyer's office, saying he wants a direct phone call from me because he has my best interest at heart. Boy, I want to be me. No.

May 18, 1994

Yet another letter from the ex came to my lawyer threatening to prosecute my lawyer on two felony charges, as did this telephone message of the ex to my lawyer May 17, 1994 7:19 p.m.:

"I tried to explain to you I needed a few minutes to talk to you, but I'll just give you the message over the phone. I have retained the, uh ... services of Terry McWilliams. He's a criminal attorney down out of Florida. He a former chief prosecutor for Janet Reno when she was the state's attorney's office.

"It appears you violated, uh, Florida Statue 91244, witness tampering, in addition you've illegally obtained attorney work product through fraud misrepresentation and that was early in the case by trying to get work product that you thought only belonged to Julia and uh, (Florida lawyer) it was my work, it was work product between (Florida Lawyer) and I too.

"Um, it appears that according to Terry, we have enough to prosecute you on two felony charges, and I did not want that to come as a surprise. Uh, Terry's preparing the stuff to present to the, uh, state's attorney's office. Also it turns out that, uh, that the, uh, police reports that Julia made with the police department are fraudulent. I can account for my time. I've taken a polygraph test to verify and got enough evidence to show that I was neither near or around her at the time the police reports were made, and I've an appointment with the district attorney in the morning, uh, and some other stuff but um. ...

"I just wanted to try to advise you since you obviously think that I am just going to go away, it just ain't gonna happen. Um, as for ah, your threatening me during the depo and what advising to, uh, you intend to see if you can get a buyer, to sell my identity since I was active with the U.S. Intelligence Agency. According to the U.S. Attorney's Office, Mike Mallany, that also appears to be a felony ? And the FBI has been advised and I have a conference call with them at uh, nine o'clock in the morning, which is twelve o'clock Miami time tomorrow to conference with the FBI Special Agent in charge of that particular area in the U.S. Attorneys...Assistant

U.S. Attorney that handles this type of thing. So please govern yourself accordingly, and hopefully I can get copies of that depo real fast, and umm, like I say, it was nice to see Julia but not under these circumstances. Goodbye."

Well, the ex is right about one thing, he won't go away. As far as his supposed identity, the ex honestly believes he is a FBI agent and works for the CIA, and a world class fighter pilot. It's scary that he is so delusional.

May 20, 1994

My lawyer wrote to the ex that he did not deem the ex's latest letter to be privileged or confidential and will request at the time of trial sanctions due to his continuing threats of criminal prosecution.

May 21, 1994

My lawyer wrote to tell me of the notices he has received about taking the depositions of my sister and brother-in-law and that actress. He told me that he thinks it is best not for him to appear as he feels that their testimonies are not relevant, of which I agree.

May 23, 1994

My lawyer sends a letter to the judge in the 17th Judicial District in Broward County that I am now in Pro Se—I am impecunious because a sizable amount on what little money I have left is now being spent on my divorce proceedings, because the ex will not cease and the recovery from the savage canine attack is my sole and separate property for the injured spouse under both California and Florida law. My lawyer tells the judge that he's not sure if the ex actually believes he is entitled to and/or will be awarded some part of the injury recovery monies or because he is obsessive about the failed marriage.

My thoughts are this: going into this marriage looked great, getting out was the worst experience of my life. Having to heal from the dog attack was just one thing, however, being a single parent and raising my son that the ex abused and molested in one 9 hour day, Valentine's Day, and doing the best I could to take care of my mother, my plate was full. My parents were married for forty years. I truly doubt I will be getting married again ever.

May 26, 1994

My lawyer responded to a letter from the ex that his deposition is being cancelled due to an accident the ex has had. My lawyer insisted the ex provide him with medical justification for the cancellation and the appropriate medical documents of when he will be able to be deposed. The ex also now has another lawyer (poor guy), and he is in receipt of yet another letter from the ex to me and reminds him he is not authorized or permitted to communicate directly with me, and if the ex does not cease and desist, restraining orders will be enforced. When?! Please, just lie to me, let me live on false hope, surely I paid enough for that.

June 2, 1994

An order from the Circuit Court of the 17th Judicial Circuit in and for Broward County hereby dismissed the Florida motions by the judge. Finally.

June 3, 1994

The Florida lawyer wrote to my lawyer that he is sorry his last letter had an ungracious tone; however, he will not represent me without the $1,085.75. My lawyer also received a letter from the judge dismissing the Florida motion and thanked him for his attention to this difficult case.

June 9, 1994

My lawyer wrote to the ex that his request for bifurcation (where something divides) and a delay of the property element of the dissolution need not follow with his pejorative comments (negative connotations to belittle) and offensive statements. My lawyer also requested fees and sanctions for his behavior, and referred to the ex's so-called serious injury by assessing that "it may be more in the richness of your imagination than the fabric of reality."

It was just another way the ex refused to respond and tried to buy more time to keep harassing me. It's evident that all he wants to do is make sure I have no money in the end by his obsessive antics at all costs.

June 10, 1994

My lawyer wrote to the Florida lawyer enclosing a copy of the Court's order dismissing the Florida dissolution action initiated by the ex. He requests the Florida lawyer to send him all copies of his bills to me, even though he didn't do anything; it was my lawyer that spoke with the Florida judge for dismissal. This really is such a mess. Shame on everybody.

June 14, 1994

My lawyer wrote a letter to the man from the mortgage company in question created on May 6, 1991, that the property (the ex's house) stands in the name of the ex, who acquired title as a single man, as the mortgage title itself recites. The ex purported to convey an interest in the property to me by Quick Claim Deed dated August 21, 1993. My lawyer's concern with the mortgage man is that he is auctioning off the ex's house and will not let it affect my credit. My lawyer also refers to the ex as "the unfortunate circumstances that I'm caught up in with the unfortunate marriage with the unfortunate ex."

You can see how the ex in the very beginning did everything possible to refer all and any outstanding bills or anything else he could think of on to me. You really have to do a lot of thinking to be so vicious. Obviously he never had a dime, just a victim—me. My lawyer is funny though.

June 15, 1994

The Florida lawyer sent a letter and all copies of statements to my lawyer and his retainer agreement from 1993 to 1994. Oh my God, thank you so much, thank you, really, you shouldn't have.

June 15, 1994

My lawyer received a letter by the ex that he will not appear for deposition and his antics had better stop. Also written in the same letter is that July 11, 1994, my lawyer has a conflict since the ex postponed his deposition again and tried to reschedule. For such a bully, he sure is afraid to step up to the plate, don't you think?

June 23, 1994

My lawyer wrote to the ex that if he wishes to continue to play out his fiction that he resides in Florida—when it's obvious that he lives, works, and whatever else he does in Southern California—he will have to bear the procedural results. If the ex does or doesn't wish to appear, fine, my lawyer doesn't wish to play his game.

Today was the ex's deposition at 10 a.m. at my lawyer's office. He was a no-show.

July 1, 1994

My lawyer wrote to me after a letter I wrote to him regarding my mother and her possessions that if we can prove the ex wrote a letter on behalf of my sister and brother-in-law that they threw her out of her add-on that she paid for and took all and any of her belongings, it will be helpful in my dissolution.

Also, the Florida lawyer again sends me his bill for $1,085.75. I'm getting right on that, because you can obviously see the results I'm getting.

CHAPTER 17 – THE END ISN'T THE END

August 9, 1994

I finally have my divorce. Wow, what a lucky girl I am. But the ex still will not stop harassing me, and I'm broke, sick, and tired, I literally came home to my son and mom and threw up. If you could have seen the ex in court, dirty with his worn-out shoes, shirt, and pants, the glare in his eyes looking at me and my lawyer and how close he tried to get to me during the trial—well, you would have to have been there.

August 16, 1994

The ex wrote to my lawyer that he is attempting to set an Ex Parte hearing on August 19, purporting to seek a restraining order against me. My lawyer told the ex he has now exceeded the bounds and that the ex obviously has personality problems. At the time of trial, he will again request restraining orders against the ex. The restraining order he requested against me was denied by the judge, and now he is in contempt of court.

My lawyer also told the ex that any dispute between my sister and brother-in-law in regard to my mother and her possessions, of which they refuse to give her, is clearly a sign of his interference with this matter. The ex using the social relationship with my sister and brother-in-law as a lever, avenue, vehicle, or instrument with molesting, harassing or otherwise involving himself in my life is a direct and express violation of the restraining order imposed against him by the court, and remedies for contempt will be sought. My lawyer added, "I believe that it is fair to say that not only I, but the Court as well are becoming fatigued and strained at his antics. I think the time has come for them to stop. If you will not stop them, or are incapable of stopping them yourself, I will ask the Court to do that for you."

Separate letters from my lawyer to the CIA and FBI August 16, 1994

Re: In re Marriage of the EX an/ Benjamin-......
L.A.S.C. West District, Case No. ....

Dear Gentleperson:

I represent Respondent, Julia Benjamin in the above captioned action for the dissolution of her marriage to the ex.

Mr. Ex had made representations, on and off the record, that he is and/or has been employed or associated with your agency, and has made further representations that your agency is cooperating with him with the respect to his civil actions against his estranged spouse, Julia Benjamin, as well as with respect to civil and possibly criminal actions against the undersigned.

I need, first, to verify that Mr. Ex is not employed with your agency, and that no employee or official of your agency, in his or her capacity as such, is working with him with the aforementioned subject matter. Second, I wish to register a complaint and ask you to investigate the matter of Mr. Ex passing himself off as an agent of the Federal Government and as an agent of the Central Intelligence Agency/ Federal Bureau of Investigation in particular, and using that status as a threat.

Your rapid attention to this matter would be greatly desired. Mr. Ex's representations that your agency is cooperating with him in connection with his actions against his estranged spouse is creating a great deal of emotional distress, and I think from the perspective of the agency, as well as from my perspective as the representative of Ms. Benjamin, the victim of Mr. Ex's actions, a quick investigation and immediate halt to these actives would be in all parties best interest.

My lawyer writes a damn good letter. I'm even interested in reading my own book. This is obviously not Ludlum's *The Borne Identity*, of course. The ex couldn't rent an identity about who or what he is in the fabric of his imagination.

August 16, 1994

The ex now has two addresses, the one in Florida and Movie Tech Inc. at 832 N. Seward St. in Hollywood, Calif. That's right down the street from the old Social Security offices where all of us in the industry, children included, would go to get our unemployment checks if our shows were cancelled or if we didn't have a job.

August 23, 1994

The ex moved for an Ex Parte Application, not allowing my lawyer enough time to travel from Laguna Beach to Santa Monica, and will request sanctions. Also, a letter was sent to my address in the ex's name from North Shore Collection Agency for $26.75 regarding an outstanding bill owed by the ex for coffee. My lawyer wrote back to the company that the ex is using my address to obtain credit and that I will have nothing to do with all of his outstanding bills.

August 29, 1994

My lawyer wrote to the judge handling my divorce that ask for a slight change in wording from "the Respondent shall pay" to "Respondent shall be responsible for the remainder of the medical bills arising out of the dog attack." The change was needed because the ex threatened to initiate contempt against me if I did not pay the bills, even though by this time I'm impecunious (broke) because of the ex and his antics.

The ex is also responsible for his own properties due to the Quick Claim deed from Florida to his house. Again, the ex has threatened my lawyer that he will receive a phone call from the federal law enforcement agencies as well as the West Los Angeles District Attorney's office as the ex is now accusing my lawyer of perjury and other crimes.

I tried right from the beginning to tell my lawyer the ex is certifiably crazy. He didn't believe me at first. In fact, he told me that he wasn't going to be in the middle of a vindictive argument between the ex and me. All I ever wanted is for the ex to leave me along and get a divorce from this monster.

August 30, 1994

My lawyer wrote back to the ex that he cannot change the judge's rulings nor control his conduct (now there's a novel statement!), and if he objected to the proposed judgment, it was not an invitation for a free-for-all attack on the court's rulings.

The court has ordered sanctions for the ex to pay me $3,750 at $300 per month beginning September 1, 1994. My lawyer tells me that he did not make the last payment.

Letter from my lawyer to the ex, September 19, 1994:

I am in receipt of your letter of Sept. 15, 1994. As I have told you many, many times in the past, the only way that you can change your address for the purpose of service of pleadings, orders and other documents is by filing with the clerk of the court and serving upon the undersigned a "Notice of Change of Address." In fact, my files indicate that at one point, I went so far as to actually draft one for you, so that you would be sure to have in the proper form. Unless and until to you file such a notice and serve it upon the undersigned, I am required to serve to your address of record, particularly with a document as important as a proposed Judgment.

As to your objections to the proposed Judgment: First, as to your objection to the restraining order, that objection is directed to the merits and substance of the Court's ruling, not to the form of the proposed Judgment. As I, made clear in my covering letter, such an objection to the substance of the Court's ruling may not be raised in this context: the only issue is whether the proposed Judgment conforms to the orders of the court. The Judge had made a ruling for the issuance of restraining order, and has specifically ordered them to be included in the judgment; accordingly your objection to the restraining order is not acceptable in the present context. Your purported "grounds" for the objection are not worthy of comment.

As to the second objection, to the "re-wording" of the Judge's Order, since you do not indicate what the nature of the objection may be, I cannot comment. It appears to me that my proposed Judgment conforms is all particulars to the letter, spirit and intent of the Court's ruling(s); if you file objections on the bases set forth in your letter, requiring further unnecessary legal work on my part to settle the Judgment, I shall ask for sanctions for my appearance and travel time.

CHAPTER 18 – FINALLY THE REAL END

September 19, 1994

Dissolution of Marriage

Restraining Order

Male 5'8" Hair Color BLD Eye Color Blue Race White Age 44 DOB blank

CHAPTER 19 - ONE MORE THING TO NOTE

Letter from the CIA October 3, 1994:

Dear My Lawyer,

We have no record of employment, either current or previous for a Mr. Ex. If Mr. Ex continues to maintain that he is or was an employee of the Central Intelligence Agency, please advise him to contact our office with additional information regarding his employment.

Sincerely,

L. Halder
Employee Services Officer

EPILOGUE

Many years after the last legal correspondence, I received a call from an extremely aggressive female detective who proceeded to tell me that my ex is now greatly in fear of his life, terrified that my son and I are going to kill him. During our conversation, I calmly explained to the detective the details of the last twenty-three years – the dog attack, his non-stop legal antics, and that my ex was basically stalking ME…walking back and forth around my Playa del Rey apartment until my son and I were forced to move to another building – a gated one, and into a third floor condo at that. That move took place about six months prior to the detective phoning me. After twenty minutes on the phone with this woman, she finally seemed to understand that it wasn't me…it was HIM. After the call, I never heard from the detective again. Paul came by right after that phone call to pick up Branden and me and take us to lunch and shopping. When I told him about the call, we were totally at a loss for words…and that was the last I heard that had anything to do with my ex.

The economic crash in 2009 hit us really hard – first we lost our car and then the new condo. We had to get used to taking the bus for four years. That's a major inconvenience in Los Angeles where a car is mandatory. In 2013, Branden and I decided to leave LA for a fresh start in Colorado. He had grown into a fine young adult, and he became a gourmet chef as his chosen profession. A serious accident at work one night resulted in Branden's legs being burned. He walked six blocks to an E.R. and didn't tell me until he got there! He was able to recover (thankfully), and he received a nice settlement thanks an honest lawyer that I hired – just enough for us to make our move. Things were starting to go our way at long last and it eventually gave me the opportunity to finally get my story in writing going.

We rented a fourteen-foot truck, packed what belongs we had left in storage and took a relaxing drive to Colorado through Las Vegas and Utah. We took our time and saw nothing but beautiful scenery along the way. It reminded me that we really do live in a beautiful country. Seeing those majestic mountains with waterfalls and natural rivers running down and underneath them was truly breathtaking. We stayed in clean, reasonably priced hotels, ate decent meals in coffee shops, swam, went shopping, and did all the things most people do when they travel leisurely. It was wonderful…and something neither of us had experienced in a very long time.

It's now two years since our move and we've never been happier. Unlike Los Angeles, everyone seems so genuine and nicer here… truly nice. My son has opened and worked in no less than three restaurants since we arrived, and I've accomplished something that has been a dream of mine for many years. You're reading it right now.

This book would not have been possible without the great help of my editor, an excellent author in his own right, pop culture expert Wesley Hyatt. Wesley went through hundreds of lawyer transcript pages and helped me organize and make sense of the last twenty-three years of my life into what you've just finished reading. I would also like to thank my friend Stu Shostak who gave the portions of this book that dealt with my early working years a real flow. Stu is a wonderful television historian and it's nice that he knows some aspects of my career better than I do.

Now, what about Hazel in the twenty-first century? Well, the season of that series that I was lucky enough to be a part of just celebrated its fiftieth anniversary. Antenna TV continues to air the reruns daily. A brand new musical stage show based on our series and on the comic strip has been playing to sold-out audiences in Chicago. Broadway appears destined on the horizon. I recently did an interview for a magazine about Shirley Booth and my experiences on the series, so it appears Hazel will live on for generations to come!

There have been many lessons I've learned throughout my roller coaster of a life. But I think the most important lesson for me is that as a single parent, no matter how difficult that challenge is (and believe me, it IS difficult), the most important person in your life is that child - never let someone else into your life to help you raise your child – it's your responsibility solely as a single parent. Second, don't be afraid to keep changing your surroundings until you find your true happiness and inner peace. For the first time in many years, my son and I are very happy. I have the best relationship with Branden right now than I have ever had. We are both survivors. When times are tough, you'll know who your best friends are and which other family members are closest to you. You'll get lots of advice, lots of criticism. But ultimately the decisions are yours. Only you can control your destiny. Yes, it takes years to figure that out, but I'm very glad that I finally did. Do I miss Hollywood? Sure. Would I go back if I was invited? Of course. Besides being right where I want to be right now, it took me a very long time to realize that the safest I have ever felt in my entire life was when we drove past that studio gate and I was on the other side.

The End.

"Susie...Ain't She A Doozie? My 'Hazel' Days and Beyond"

www.ingramcontent.com/pod-product-compliance
Lightning Source LLC
Chambersburg PA
CBHW070753100426
42742CB00012B/2115